5255

THE EXCITING WORLD OF
JACKIE STEWART

COLLINS
GLASGOW & LONDON

The Scottish Educational Trust wishes to thank all
those who have contributed so generously to this
book: Sean Connery, Hunter Davies, Eric
Dymock, Graham Gauld, Alistair MacLean, Hugh
McIlvanney, Jackie Stewart, Stuart Turner and
Ken Tyrrell.

The Trust also wishes to thank the
photographic departments of Dunlop, Elf, Ford
and Goodyear for providing the pictures. Finally,
grateful thanks are due to Jeremy Walton for all
his help and advice.

First published 1974
Published by William Collins Sons & Co. Ltd.,
Glasgow and London

Designed and edited by Youé & Spooner Ltd.

Printed in Great Britain by Flarepath Printers Ltd.
ISBN 0 00 106183 6 (paperback)
ISBN 0 00 106182 8 (cased)

Contents

Foreword

by Sean Connery

I can't remember when or where I met Jackie. Perhaps it was during the Depression in the Labour Exchange queue! Anyway, he is the sort of person I feel I've known all my life. One reason for this is that there are parallels between his life and mine: we both left Scotland before we became successful, and our lives have been especially similar in the way the world has looked on our 'Scottishness'.

Scottishness is a difficult quality to pin down — later in the book Hunter Davies makes a good attempt to do so — but it is something strong in both Jackie and myself. Both of us, for instance, are trustees of the Scottish International Educational Trust which was set up three years ago with myself as one of its founder members, and Jackie has donated any profits he is making from the present book to the Trust.

So the Trust is important for both of us, mainly because it actually *gets things done* for people in Scotland. The trustees are one reason for this: they must form one of the most diverse and powerful groups of Scots anywhere in the world.

They range from Sir Samuel Curran, now Principal of Strathclyde University and at one time Britain's chief atomic scientist, to Alastair Dunnett, former editor of the *Scotsman*, and Sir Iain Stewart (another Stewart!), Chairman of such companies as The Dorchester Hotel and Beaverbrook Newspapers, and much admired in Scotland for his recent fight to save Fairfields Shipyard in Govan.

All these people, and others, regularly put a good deal of work into the Trust, with the express aim of promoting individual talent, from wherever it stems, which might serve to promote Scotland's name. The list of all those who have received money from the Trust is a long one, but they stretch from people in the worlds of sport and music to others who have made studies on workers' self-management or on the impact of North Sea Oil developments. So there is plenty of diversity. And when we invited Jackie Stewart on to the Trust he agreed enthusiastically, since when he has been one of its foremost members.

Strangely enough, despite some of the machines I found myself driving in my James Bond days, I am no motor racing fanatic. In 1973, however, I decided to accept Jackie's invitation to join him, together with a few friends, at Silverstone, where Ford and Jackie were hosts for the day. All strapped in and helmeted, I was taken round the circuit — with Jackie driving. Generally, I would say that his judgment and realistic approach to life are two of his strongest points. He once told me that, when racing down the straight, he could discern faces in the crowd and found that, when he was no longer able to distinguish them, that was the time to slow down. All the same, even in normal circumstances I am a bad passenger and much prefer to do the driving: I frequently drive my chauffeur to and from the studios. But being driven at 140 mph, in spite of my driver being the world's champion, was quite the most frightening experience in my life.

When we screeched into the bends Jackie would calmly explain the technicalities of what he was doing, yet his voice was like a fly buzzing round my head while inside me there was a great thumping noise like a bass drum. Only afterwards did I realize it was my heart! When I staggered out of the car I was positive that nothing would ever get me on to that track again, yet within ten minutes I was back — driving solo. So it was through Jackie's encouragement that I realized the thrill of speed — and I can quite easily see myself now doing a 'Walter Mitty' and taking up motor racing. Just whether that day will ever come, we shall have to see.

Racing fever

The speed, the noise, the smell, the roar of the crowd — once addicted to these, you have a disease for which there is no known cure. Alistair MacLean, whose thriller, *The Way to Dusty Death,* has as its climax a motor-racing duel, sets out to examine the sport's strange fascination

The atmosphere in the pits is tense as mechanics uncover the cars and attend to last-minute details. Then the button is pressed and they're off. Jackie Stewart, with all four wheels of his Matra-Ford off the ground, hurtles down the straight during the 1969 German Grand Prix

There's an American from Butte, Montana, who makes a great deal of money from performing acts on a motor cycle that should, one would have thought, automatically have qualified him for immediate and forcible incarceration in the nearest lunatic asylum.

He specializes in taking himself — and, naturally, his motorcycle — very long distances through the air, usually in the most dangerous circumstances imaginable. He has set a world record by jumping over twenty parked cars. He has taken his machine some 140 feet across the fountains at Caesar's Palace in Las Vegas. He has soared across a volcanic crater and, on this occasion, just to add a soupçon of excitement to the performance, he had the crater filled with rattlesnakes while he landed on the far side in a narrow lane between two rows of lions. But those are but the veriest kindergarten ploys compared to what he intends to do this summer at Snake River Gorge in Idaho.

He has had a ramp constructed on one edge of the gorge, and it is his declared intent to mount this ramp at 350 mph and land on the far bank one full mile away. Some of the experiments he has carried out have been less than encouraging. On the last one, a test machine with a dummy rider aboard took off in splendid style, got half-way across, then plunged like the proverbial stone 600 vertical feet, which is the depth of the gorge. In spite of this thought-provoking setback, Mr Evel Knievel — for such is his name — remains undeterred, although he philosophically accepts the fact that, in all probability, he will end up plastered against the far wall of the canyon. Yet to a man the bookmakers of Las Vegas do not concede that there is even the possibility of a probability; none will consider even the most astronomical odds offered.

Mr Knievel has broken every bone in his body — although his neck, I understand, remains intact. Why does he do it? He exhibits no coyness about his reasons — or reason. He does it solely for money. He claims to have made more of it than any other athlete in history, and expects to make not less than a million pounds for his forthcoming Idaho exploit.

And why does he make so much money? Mr Knievel is in no two minds. His opinion of his fellow man is not high. He reckons that human nature has not changed a whit since the days of the Roman gladiatorial games, and that there will always be those happily prepared to part with good money to see a man dice spectacularly with death. The fact that Mr Knievel is a major contributor to the furtherance of this moral turpitude does not appear to have occurred to him or, if it has, he has performed a heroic task in repressing his pangs of conscience. However, that is not relevant: his opinion is.

In 1936, the most popular song was a waltz called When I grow too old to dream. This was at the time of a particular savage and brutal murder case, and the song that grew up around it, which received wide and popular acceptance, was called When you grow too old

8

to scream, I'll have you to dismember. This sickness of mind reveals itself in many ways, although finding explanations is less easy. Why this obsessive interest, for instance, in murder and murder trials, the gorier the better? Thousands more are killed on the roads every year than are murdered, but who cares about them? When the giant DC-10 crashed north of Paris, carrying all 345 aboard to their deaths, so many thousands of people congregated on the scene in so incredibly short a time that police and army operations were rendered extremely difficult.

What motivates such ghoulish rubberneckers? Why do well-dressed and presumably well-bred ladies scream with excitement at the ringside as they watch a pugilist beating his opponent into something close to a bloody

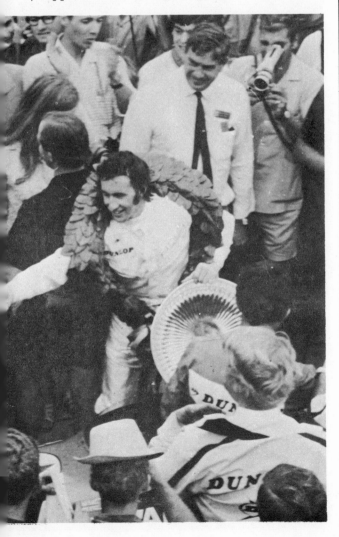

pulp? Why all this compulsive obsession with violence, and viciously detailed violence at that, on television and the big screen? Why bullfighting, which the Spanish (whom I don't believe) claim to have elevated to a fine art form? Why do people hide in remote valleys and deserted back lots and watch steel-taloned fighting cocks rip each other to pieces? Why Oscar Wilde's unspeakable in pursuit of the uneatable — the fox-hunters — whose hunting jackets are perhaps not coincidentally coloured red?

The mind of man is a many-faceted thing, and some of the facets detailed above — and they are all basically the same — are not particularly pretty. Is this primeval blood-lust — for that is what it is all about — an ineradicable factor of human nature? If so, what and how much does it have to do with racing fever?

I have been to Formula 1 Grand Prix races but make no claim to being a devoted afficionado. Whether this necessarily leads to a detached viewpoint or a properly judicial consideration, I do not know. I just know that I am not conscious of any deep involvement.

That there are those who turn up at the Grand Prix tracks of the world in the anticipation of seeing a racing car crash into a wall — or better still into another car — at speeds of anything up to 200 mph, with the concomitant bursting of fuel tanks and blazing white flames from the magnesium alloy wheels, I do not for a moment doubt. If a driver is killed or burnt to death, all the better reason for the arms to be held high in hypocritical horror — and it is an unfortunate fact that occasions for the expression of this horror occur with dismaying frequency.

For the dedicated ghoul, the opportunities for the expression of his blood-lust come in an endless variety of permutations, ranging from a pleasantly spine-chilling thrill when a car goes into a dangerous skid to a kind of inverted religious ecstasy when the zenith of his twisted ambitions have been realized in a multiple pile-up from which, preferably, no one emerges unscathed.

I have known, slightly, a few racing drivers — one well enough to call a friend — and they are unanimous in their opinion that such a maniacal element does exist. As those most intimately concerned, they are singularly un-appreciative of this attitude of mind. This *morituri te salutamus* syndrome has no appeal of any kind for them. They do not visualize themselves in the roles of latter-day gladiators, using enormously horse-powered cars for weapons instead of sword, net and trident for the edification of a Roman bread-and-circuses mob. Each of them wants just to be first past the finishing post — without, if possible, so much as scratching his own paint, or that of any of his competitors.

Statistics, of course, are impossible to come by. Few, if any, of us are possessed of Uri Geller's alleged ability to read minds but those same drivers are convinced that the sadistic element constitutes only a tiny fraction of the viewing public. I am sure they are right, and that the hypnotic attraction of motor racing — especially Grand Prix racing — lies elsewhere.

A Grand Prix driver once said to me: 'I have a beautiful wife, beautiful children and a beautiful home' — and he unquestionably has all of those — 'but life really starts for me when I push that button.' I doubt whether he still holds that view, but I do not doubt that he meant it at the time he said it.

For this is where the greatest appeal of motor racing lies. It brings out a greater degree of audience participation and total involvement than any other sport I know. Life also starts for the crowd when that button is pressed. In fact, it is they who press the button, for it is in this admittedly highly dangerous but indisputably glamorous sport that Walter Mitty comes into his own. Here hero-worship reaches its summit, a totally committed empathy its peak.

The Stewarts, the Hills, the Fittipaldis may believe they are driving alone, but they couldn't be further wrong. Each is accompanied by thousands of devoted and concerned co-drivers — no small feat, granted, in a tailor-made cockpit — who change gears whenever he changes gears, brake when he

Chris Amon in number 28 leads Jackie Stewart, number 21 and Jacky Ickx, number 26, at the start of the 1970 Monaco Grand Prix

Jim Clark in number 3 leads at the start of the 1967 German Grand Prix, above. In number 2 is Denny Hulme, who eventually won the race, leading Jackie Stewart in number 11. Below, Jackie Stewart in a BRM leads Dan Gurney who eventually overtook him to win the 1967 Belgian Grand Prix

brakes, overtake when he overtakes and help him corner to the limit of adhesion. Many of the more critically minded co-drivers are probably of the opinion that they could do better themselves, but that does not alter their worshipful admiration of the young and sometimes not-so-young — *pace* Graham Hill — demi-gods behind the wheel. They're with him there all the way, never more so than during those nail-biting moments when he's out of sight on the other side of the course. Far from any blood-lust being in his mind, the co-driver devoutly wishes him well. For he's in that car too.

Next in importance to the participation factor is the one of competition. Competition, after all, is the *raison d'être* of sport. Crowds don't jam football stadiums in the hope of witnessing a blood-bath. Although a miniscule section may be incurable hoodlums, their minds are not necessarily filled with the longing for blood; they are just bloody-minded, which is a different thing entirely. They are there for the competition. Rod Laver and John Newcombe do not regard the tennis court as a jousting ground where honour demands that they belabour each other over their heads with a tennis racket: they go out to compete.

Spassky and Fischer have never — to the best of my knowledge — been known to hurl chessmen at each other, but they held much of the civilized world spellbound during their world championship encounter in Iceland. They were — all too obviously — just competing.

And there cannot be a more demandingly competitive sport in the world than motor racing. It *is* the most competitive sport in the world. In most other sports, one has either team versus team or individual versus individual. Here every individual is up against every other individual, with the result that one does not have just one contest but many contests. The dicing between cars lying seventh and eighth may be just as enthralling as the duel for first place. And in no other sport do fortunes change so rapidly, with advantages being gained and lost with such bewildering speed, and to the accompaniment of an almost unbearable tension and excitement.

Inseparable from the competitive element is that of skill. As with the first two factors, here motor racing surely stands alone. There are many excellent footballers, cricket players, basketball players and players in a dozen other sports in the world, but there are not many excellent racing drivers. Though there may be

anything up to 24 Formula 1 Grand Prix drivers, the truly great ones can be counted on one's fingers — and if one were to lose the odd finger or thumb the assertion would still stand. Those few drive their machines — and themselves — to the utter limit, where a fraction error, a tiny percentage in judgment can quite literally mark that shadowy boundary between life and death.

The closest one can get to this factor of ice-cold judgment is to see a Mike Hailwood lean his motor bike over to an amazing angle of 57 degrees as he rounds a corner. But somehow motor cycling does not command the immense public following that motor racing does. In any event, all we can do is watch in sad envy, knowing that it is a capacity that will forever lie beyond our reach, our immortals of the sport displaying skills that border on the supernatural.

Then, of course, comes the factor of sheer speed. The spectacle of a Grand Prix car passing in a blinding blur as it hurtles along the long straight at Le Mans at something in excess of 200 mph cannot fail to stir even the most blasé. Speed has always fascinated man — and motor racing is the fastest sport on earth.

All those elements — involvement, competition, skill and speed — are essential to the understanding of racing fever, because in no other sport are any of the four so splendidly exemplified. But there are three other factors that contribute to motor racing's pre-eminence among sports.

There is the factor of noise. The shattering roar of an eight-cylinder Ford-Cosworth engine accelerating up to maximum revolutions is an auditory experience never to be forgotten, especially when it is accompanied by the screaming of tyres as the sliding car comes out of a corner. There is the unmistakable smell of hot oil, of burnt high octane fuel, of burnt rubber and dust. And, always, there is the roar of the crowd. To all of those things the vast majority of racing enthusiasts become quickly and permanently addicted.

I think the word 'addiction' sums it up. Grand Prix motor racing is concerned with the blood all right, but not with blood-lust: it is a disease of the blood for which there appears to be no known cure.

Great Scot!

Hunter Davies is a Scotsman whose writings in the *Sunday Times* have made him justly famous. Yet he envies the Scottish kids who have grown up in the last ten years. They have had a genuine, tartan paid-up Scottish hero to worship, one acknowledged by the world as a truly great. But what does it mean to be a Scotsman in the motor-racing world and how much of the Scotsman is left in Stewart now?

If you love Wee Wullie and The Broons then you're Scottish and of indeterminate age. If Tammy Troot starts a tingle or Down at the Mains sends a shiver, or if you remember Jimmy Logan saying 'Sausages is the boys', or if your hero was ever Billy Houlison, then you'll be determinedly Scottish and you'll be aged something over 30.

Being Scottish, like being part of any other national minority, means having folk heroes outsiders can never understand. They give you a glow. You feel special.

Outsiders probably don't want that sort of glow. They don't mind not being special. They could say, quite rightly, that you must be a bit retarded if you're over seven and *still* love Wee Wullie and the other comic characters from the *Sunday Post*. Tammy Troot was a fish who was the hero of a children's series on the old steam radio. As comedians' catch phrases go, there can't have been a more pointless one than Jimmy Logan's. And as for Billy Houlison, he was a bull-neck centre forward with no noticeable skill who managed to score some vital goals for Scotland and we were all duly prostrate with gratitude.

They were all my heroes. Someone like Billy Houlison was a super-hero because he helped to defeat the dreaded English. I filled scrap-book after scrap-book with his soggy, cold-paste, ink-impregnated face. I had cuttings

Jackie Stewart's tartan-blazoned crash helmet, Beatles cap and Royal Blue car sporting the cross of St Andrew became familiar throughout the world

from countless pink 'uns and green 'uns sent to me from Cambuslang, where my father's family lived, and from Motherwell, where my mother had come from. We were living in Dumfries at the time, so the devotion was extra special. Mr Houlison played for the local team, Queen of the South. Wow!

When I was ten we moved over the border to Carlisle, among the enemy English. We resolutely took the *Sunday Post* and the Scottish *Daily Express* and listened only to the Scottish BBC. Scottish news is always so much nicer. I joined the Church of Scotland Boy Scouts and never went bike rides on Sundays, always picked brummles not blackberries, went tatie howking not tatie picking, ate champers not spuds, had a jittering bite after swimming not a jam buttie, went back to the hoose not yam, longed to go Doon the Watter, not to Blackpool; but it wasn't the same. The lads sniggered when I flashed my soggy Billy Houlisons. They couldn't believe in Tammy Troot. I longed for a real Scottish hero, one they would have to acknowledge as being a truly great Scot.

I envy all those Scottish kids who've been growing up these last ten years. They've had Jackie Stewart to hang on to: a real, genuine, tartan paid-up, full-size, *world* hero.

Is he the greatest living Scotsman? Sean Connery's face must be better known, thanks to James Bond, but Mr Connery on film speaks Hollywood-Edinburgh and his public image is certainly not Scottish. Sir Alec Douglas-Home has been Prime Minister but it would be hard to make a case for him as the greatest living Scotsman. There's Billy Bremner whose drive and enthusiasm helped Scotland to the 1974 World Cup. But soccer, alas, is still virtually unknown in the United States. Mary Stewart, the romantic novelist, has often been number one in the US, and so has Alistair MacLean, another brand leader. But it's hard for popular writers ever to be called great, even if they manage a world audience. Lulu and Stanley Baxter, as popular entertainers, have still not managed the flickerings of a world audience.

Sir Robert Watson-Watt, the inventor of radar, has recently died. In fact, all the truly *great* Scotsmen seem to be dead, and long dead at that — James Watt, Robert Burns, Walter Scott, Andrew Carnegie, Robert Louis Stevenson, Thomas Carlyle, Alexander Fleming, Logie Baird. No doubt Dr Johnson would say that the only good Scotsmen are dead Scotsmen . . .

While we wait for the next Scottish genius to invent something amazing, write a masterpiece, or even just make a lot of money (the three ways in which great Scotsmen usually show their greatness), let us appraise John Young Stewart.

He's definitely Scottish. Throughout his career as the world champion racing driver he was even *defiantly* Scottish. His car was Royal Blue and sported the cross of St Andrew. His tartan-blazoned crash helmet became familiar throughout the world. It was his wife, Helen McNeil McGregor from Helensburgh (how's that for a real Scots lass?) who first pinned that strip of tartan on his helmet at a race at Charterhall in 1961. She chose a piece of Royal Stewart tartan, though Hunting Stewart would have been more appropriate for a sportsman. As a boy Jackie had always worn a Royal Stewart kilt. His big brother, Jimmy, had the Hunting Stewart kilt, just to keep them different.

They lived near the family garage in Dumbarton with great views looking over the Clyde. ('An uninterrupted view, except for two roads and two railway lines.') They took their holidays, like all good Scottish families, at Rothesay, staying in a rather posh hydro, the Glenburn, as the garage was usually doing rather well. For day trips, like everyone else, they went down the water from the Broomielaw, on the Waverley or the Jeanie Deans. For a special night out, Jackie was taken into Glasgow to see Harry Gordon at the Alhambra.

'As a kid I definitely felt Scottish, but in Scotland you don't have to come from a nationalist family to feel that. You just sense that England is somehow against you, that everything is centred on London and that Scotland misses out.

'I couldn't say I was football daft like the other kids. I didn't come from a football daft family, but I listened to every Scottish match on the radio and I loved to hear the Hampden

Jackie Stewart reckons that much of his and Jim Clark's success as racing drivers can be attributed to their Scottishness. 'Scots are canny,' he says. 'They don't act impetuously but at the same time they're very determined, very stubborn'

Roar. You never hear of the Wembley Roar, do you? I loved Our Wullie. I always read him first before The Broons. He was the individualist, the loner — that appealed to me.'

He went to Dumbarton Academy, a rather smart local grammar school, which was fee-paying when he first started but soon became public. (In Scotland, public means public and open to all.) He wasn't much good at lessons and left at fifteen to work on his dad's petrol pumps.

He began to venture over the border in 1963, as a young racing driver, and thought himself very much the provincial hick, convinced the smart English were looking down on him.

'I felt I had bits of haggis and twigs of heather growing out of my ears. All the people I met at the English motor clubs seemed so sophisticated in every way. I *had* to win to prove I was as good as them. I loved winning English pound notes and taking them back to Scotland.'

When at last he hit London, making that his base for a full-time assault on English pound notes, he was lucky. Jim Clark, a fellow Scotsman, had not only opened up the trail as a driver, but had the social entrée ready and waiting. Sir John Whitmore, a well-known amateur racing driver, was a personal friend of Jim Clark and he'd opened his Mayfair flat to Clark, Stewart and other visiting Scotsmen.

'We called it the Scottish Embassy. It meant I didn't have to get to know London on my own as an outsider. Jim Clark was then the champion Formula 1 driver and I was coming up in Formula 3.'

Very soon Jackie was into Formula 1, coming second in Grand Prix races to Clark. By the time Clark was killed in 1968, Jackie had established himself as world champion material. For eleven years, from 1962-1973, all World Championship Grand Prix races were dominated by the two Scotsmen, a heady time for all British racing fans and for chauvinistic Scotsmen everywhere. Physically they were similar — short, strong and lithe, with powerful forearms. But was there anything special in their Scottishness?

'I think so. Scots are canny, they don't rush in. They digest the whole position and don't act impetuously. They don't take risks and seldom gamble. At the same time, they're very determined, very stubborn, never give up. Those are all good attributes for a racing driver.

'Basically, I think Scots are pessimists. They never say, "I'm going to win that." I always thought the opposition was superior to me. I had a fear of the opposition, not a fear of death. Perhaps the Scots do have an inferiority complex, whatever they say about being better than the English.

'I was always conscious in all my races that I was racing as a Scotsman, racing for Scotland. I remember the Canadian Grand Prix in 1971. Jimmy had never won it and neither had I, yet we'd always had thousands of exiled Scots cheering us. I felt I'd cheated them.

'I won it that year. Afterwards, I locked myself as usual in my caravan to recover, to wait for the crowds to go home. It was a very foggy day and I'll always remember it. I eventually came out to go home and was walking through the fog with Edsel Ford, Henry Ford's son. We came to this lock-up wooden hut, half hidden in mist, and as we went past, we could hear someone inside playing Amazing Grace on the bagpipes. I'd always trained myself to have no emotion during a race. I drained myself of all feelings. It was a self-taught process. I never allowed anything to interfere. Even after a race, I'd have no feelings for several hours. But listening to that bloke in the hut playing bagpipes in old, white overalls with a tamo-shanter on his head, it all flooded out. I had tears in my eyes. He'd pricked the bubble I'd enclosed myself in.

'He told me he'd tried to get on to the victory rostrum after the race, but they'd stopped him, so he'd gone back to his hut. I met him later at Watkins Glen in the States. This time he got inside and piped me into my car. I didn't want him there. I was fighting all emotion. But again tears came to my eyes as the skirl of the piper echoed in Watkins Glen. What single English thing could have the effect of the bagpipes?'

Today, having retired in 1973 as World Champion at the age of 34, he doesn't look Scottish — if it's possible for anyone actually to look Scottish without having haggis on the ear-

lobes. He always seems to have a tan, the sort of tan famous people acquire without going in the sun. It's called the glow of affluence.

It was breakfast time in one of those international jet hotels (The Carlton Tower in London) which might be anywhere, and he was wearing a pure white polo neck, hand-made crocodile shoes, a heavy gold watch and a gold ring. He too might easily have come from anywhere in the Western world. His hair is long, normal for his age though still unusual in the tweedier motor club circles. He'd been with his wife to Annabel's the night before ('the best night club in the world'), where he'd met many of his sophisticated London friends

As world champion racing driver, Jackie Stewart met people from many different worlds: top with Prince Rainer and Princess Grace after his victory in the 1973 Monaco Grand Prix, centre with Arnold Palmer at Troon and below with Princess Alexandra at the 1971 Motor Show in London

and admirers — a long way from earning £3 a week on the petrol pumps in Dumbarton.

He was about to fly back to his home in Geneva where he now lives and has his being in grounds of over six acres with a speed boat and other millionaire's toys. He uses the word 'sophisticated' a lot when referring to his lifestyle. It's the right one. People in Scotland would certainly describe him as sophisticated. He was once a fashion leader, with his Beatles cap and long hair, but now he's retired from day-to-day fashion and taken a life peerage in sophistication. The dafter forms of London High Fashion, as he must have noticed as he passed through that day, had long since moved on from long hair and as for crocodile shoes, my dear, how quaint. What one must now realize about Mr Stewart is that he is no longer Scottish or even British but international, one of those peculiar jet-set, placeless, dateless, internationals whose wealth places them beyond fashion, above nationality, almost beyond reality.

He could have had several cushy years after his retirement, traipsing round the world and doing little more than turning up and signing his name. He was reputedly earning a fortune in his last few years as champion, and it wouldn't have been too difficult to have kept most of that going for a few years by judicious endorsements and appearances.

He's taken four jobs, three of them in the motor and allied trades. He says these three are *real* jobs, not sinecures. For Ford he tests new developments. For Elf, the French International Oil firm, he does marketing, and for Goodyear he's a PR man. Whatever he says about their being real jobs, they don't sound too unexpected or too arduous. His fourth job is with the US TV Company, ABC, for whom he works as a sports commentator. He still travels 450,000 miles by aeroplane a year. That's retirement.

It's when you hear him speak, having been homogenized by his European looks and lifestyle, that you realize somewhere inside there's a Scot — whether struggling to get out or be kept in is hard to say. His strong Scottish accent is one of the clues to his American TV work.

'I got the job not just because I'm an ex-champion, but because of my voice. It's why they like the English tones of Henry Longhurst talking about golf. They like a Scottish voice on racing. It makes a change from the slick American voices. There are also twenty million people of Scottish descent in America. That helps.'

There are a few prominent examples of Scotia chic in his Geneva house. In his lounge, for example, there's a large painting of Loch Lomond. He likes to point out Ben Lomond and the other mountains, ones he went past on day trips as a boy. There's a grouse moor scene which looks like Glencoe. Elsewhere he has four paintings by George Houston. Beside the main fireplace is a huge sword he bought in Edinburgh, said to have been wielded at Culloden. What's a Scottish lad like him doing in a place like Geneva?

'It's the geographical centre of Europe. I had to be here when I was racing and it is still the most convenient place to fly from. All the same, I don't think I could go back to living in Scotland in the foreseeable future.'

Helen, for her part, says she still gets a lump in the throat when she hears the bagpipes, but it doesn't make her rush home. Her Scottish accent is fading fast and she feels herself completely European. She misses Scottish plain bread (she is the daughter of a bakery owner) and British TV, but that's about all.

They have a Scottish nanny for their two boys, Paul and Mark, and a Scottish secretary. They haven't become Swiss citizens and, if the subject ever comes up, they say they still look upon themselves as Scottish.

The previous afternoon in London, he'd been to see his English tailor, Dougie Hayward. By chance Jimmy Logan was there as well. (One of the perks of being famous is that you can meet mythological figures like Mr Logan in the flesh.) The tailor happened to say: 'Isn't it great, we're in the World Cup?'

'You should have heard Jimmy Logan. He exploded. He gave him a fifteen-minute lecture on how it was Scotland and Scotland alone who were in the World Cup. It was no use English people trying to cash in by suddenly saying Scotland was a British team. When you lose, you're Scottish, when you win, you're British. They said that about Celtic. I had it all the time when I was racing. I've lots of letters in my scrap-book from Scotsmen on that very subject. The English press always do it. But it doesn't upset me. I think it's amusing.

'I'm not a nationalist. I'm Scottish but I'm also British and proud of it. Nationalism is totally wrong for the world of the future. We can't afford the privilege. There would be far less trouble in the world if nationalism was lessened. I remember as a kid the nationalists blowing up post boxes in Scotland. That was bad enough. Now look at Ireland.

'I project my Scottishness and always will. I love going back there, going for Motor Show dinners on an old boat moored on the Clyde.

Princess Anne attended Jackie Stewart's retirement dinner given by Ford at which the guests wore the famous J.S. caps and sunglasses

They're always no-nonsense affairs, very basic and Scottish, not at all sophisticated. I love them. What I keep away from are any nationalistic elements. All over the world, wherever I went, I got invited by local Scottish societies. I didn't have time to go to many meetings, but even so I was always careful of anything too extreme. Piping in the haggis, that's fine. But nothing political.

'I often get depressed when I go back to Scotland today. It's their attitude to industry that really depresses me, especially in the central belt. I blame it on bad management. Scots are indeed canny and careful but they can fall into stodginess. Many firms don't expand because they're scared or unwilling to diversify. Look at shipping. You just can't keep on turning out ships for a hundred years. Until recently, there were enough ship-yards on the Clyde with the capacity, when working full-out, to supply the whole world. It was stupid. The demand had gone but nobody seemed to see. They all kept on till they ate themselves up. It takes new ideas and new brains to make a firm expand or diversify — and new brains don't always come from the sons of the chairman.

One of the curses of Scotland has been ingrown family firms.

'But the biggest single thing I don't like about Scotland and never liked when I was there, is the religious warring. You don't hear about it so much, not now with Ulster, but it's all there. You still find Protestant firms that won't employ Catholics. At our school we were meant to compete to the end with the boys from St Patricks. If a Catholic mother caught her daughter going out with a Protestant boy, it was the end of the world. The venom and antagonism is still there. I think it's deplorable, disgusting.

'They can be small-minded, the Scots. I hope they don't go all bombastic about having got North Sea Oil. They could oversell themselves, push too hard, which people will remember for many decades afterwards. They must find the power to see themselves as others see them, as Burns said.'

He feels no Celtic melancholy in his soul, which is lucky for him. He never gets depressed, neither is he assuaged by the thought of John Knox admonishing his actions.

'I only ever feel guilt when I'm too long away from the family. I probably spend more time at home than the normal father, but it's not enough for me.'

He has a Scotsman's carefulness with money.

(There are no mean Scotsmen, just careful.) Despite being a millionaire, he never knowingly *wastes* a penny.

'The speed boat was a gift, otherwise I'd have carried on hiring one, as it's cheaper. I could easily buy my own plane — if anyone could justify one, doing the mileage I do, then it's me. But I can't bring myself to do it. I spend a lot, especially on my home, but I don't call that wasteful. On the whole, I'd say I am canny.

'I worked hard to set up my four new jobs because, deep down, I don't really feel secure. I think that's a trait of most Scotsmen. Being successful is not the same as being secure. I didn't want to live on what I already have. I want today to pay for itself not to live off yesterday. That might be Scottish, or it could be simply being immature and juvenile . . .

'I do have this puritanical thing about not wasting time, about being busy, doing something every day. I've had incredible demands on my time since I retired, rushing round the world, having farewell banquets, collecting trophies, as well as working at the four new jobs. I've never stopped.

'But I'm still looking for something, a new passion in life. I don't have to set the heather on fire, not this time. I'd want to succeed, naturally, being a competitive person, but not necessarily to win. I now know there are deeper satisfactions than winning. What I want is something to *consume* me. Strangely enough, my first sport, clay pigeon shooting, consumed me more than motor racing. By comparison, that came easy. But where am I going to find a new all-consuming passion?'

Well, Scotland is there, waiting for him. He could move back and be Rector of every Scottish university if he wanted to. He would make a good king of the new triumphant Scottish Nationalists — he's got the right, royal Scottish surname. He is twice as dashing as Bonnie Prince Charlie, and he's got money. If Clement Freud can become an MP from such a different world, so can Jackie Stewart. He is a great talker and persuader. He has also already involved himself in a number of Scottish charities. Scotland would definitely like to take him up. But how seriously does Jackie Stewart now want to take up Scotland?

The early Jackie Stewart

What was he like in his early days and what led him into motor racing? Graham Gauld, Jim Clark's biographer, and for years a close associate of Stewart's, traces the retired champion's career

Writers and commentators the world over are always searching for the 'real' Jackie Stewart. I sometimes get the feeling that Jackie Stewart was invented by Hollywood and selected by Central Casting, yet, if the truth be told, Hollywood could never film the Jackie Stewart story for fear of having a flop on their hands: no one would believe it was true.

Perhaps the best way to describe Jackie Stewart is to give illustrations of his character at different stages in his career and see how his whole approach to racing and life has changed — as it must for any great sportsman.

Jackie was born in Milton, Dunbartonshire, on 11 June 1939. Milton is little more than a name on the map, with the bustling county town of Dumbarton a mile away and the cackle of the geese which guard the vast stocks of Ballantine's Scotch Whisky nearby. The Stewart family were something of country stock, Jackie's grandfather becoming game-keeper to Lord Weir on his estates in Dun-bartonshire. It was here that the family's genuine love of hunting, shooting and fishing began. Today you can still find Jackie up to his waist in the Spey expertly casting for salmon, or his brother Jimmy out on the Kilpatrick Hills bagging a few grouse.

Jackie's father might have followed in his father's footsteps, but he wanted to start selling motor cars, and the late Lord Weir helped him to get started in the garage business. The garage was set up on the main Glasgow-Loch Lomond road, so that there was considerable passing trade to keep the pumps busy. The

As a child, Jackie Stewart wanted to be a football player but after leaving school at the age of fifteen he began work at the family garage in Dumbarton, where he is pictured top. It was his older brother, Jimmy, pictured with him top centre, who inspired his interest in motor racing and soon he was attending race meetings in Scotland and then participating in the races. He ventured over the border in 1963 and is pictured left setting off that year for Brands Hatch to drive a Tojeiro Buick Coupe for Ecurie Ecosse, right with Graham Hill at Goodwood in 1965 and above at Le Mans in 1966

company prospered and held agencies for Austin and later Jaguar, and the Stewarts at Dumbuck had an enviable reputation in the area.

Jackie's elder brother, Jimmy, was seven years old when Jackie was born and, among other things, was a choir boy in the local church. Jackie was not to follow suit: he was more interested in football, and wanted at first to be a football player. By the time Jackie was twelve, Jimmy, who was learning the sales side of the business, had started racing and hill climbing in Scotland, and had had some success with a Healey Silverstone. David Murray of Ecurie Ecosse approached Bob Stewart, Jackie's father, and suggested that Jimmy should join them. Jimmy's father took up the idea and actually bought the C-type Jaguar that Jimmy drove under the Ecurie Ecosse banner.

Jimmy Stewart was a good racing driver who was low on luck. He twice broke the same arm and, on advice from the doctors, gave up a very promising racing career. He had driven factory Aston Martins and Jaguars, and had done well in a Cooper-Bristol in Grand Prix events. Meanwhile, Jackie watched all this from the pits and, seeing his mother's anguish at Jimmy's racing, he realized that it would be difficult for him to take the same road.

He turned his attention instead to clay pigeon shooting and soon became one of the finest shots in Britain. Indeed, the trials for the 1960 Olympics brought one of his biggest disappointments when, almost certain of a place in the two-man team, he shot off-par and lost his place. Some idea of the determination which was to mark his career in later years was demonstrated after these trials as he proceeded to go out and win everything in sight. Although he was reserve for the Rome Olympics, he determined to make the 1964 Olympics. But motor racing intervened.

Today he admits that, during his late teens, when he was enjoying a reputation as one of Britain's leading clay pigeon shots, he let himself become big-headed. Very early in his motor racing career people were making the same criticism. But, as anyone will tell you who has come to the top in one sport and then switched to another, there develops an inner

confidence which can look like conceit. I doubt if even Jackie realized how good he was as a driver until much later in his motor racing career.

Jackie Stewart has also been criticized for his hard-headedness as a businessman. But he admitted very early in his racing career that, while he enjoyed motor racing, he began to race professionally to build up a bank balance. His reasoning for this was simple. He was the younger of two brothers in the small but successful family business, and he saw that any money he made in the business would have to be ploughed back. Motor racing was a way of earning a small bank balance of his own.

The most controversial side of Jackie Stewart is still his business activities, and his earnings lead to endless speculation. The young man who started motor racing to pad out his bank-book could probably found his own modest bank. Indeed, one local wag in Scotland remarked that Stewart no longer banks his money with the Royal Bank of Scotland — the Royal Bank now banks with him!

Stewart is shrewd and always has been. He has always been willing to take advice and has rarely been wrong in choosing his advisers. Today, for instance, he is an important cog in Mark McCormack's international sports team. His earnings are therefore related to his market value. Yet when Stewart gets involved with a company on a promotion he's not just a pretty face, he works hard for his money.

He couldn't log up half a million miles a year simply through motor racing. At least half that mileage is used to back up his contracts with various companies both inside and outside motoring. He may open a motor show in one town, but you can be sure that he has probably tied in a promotion with Rolex or Goodyear or Ford in that same town. Stewart tries not to oversell himself. He takes a close

Jackie Stewart's love of fishing and shooting started very early in his life and by the time he was in his late teens he was one of Britain's leading clay pigeon shots

interest in the companies he joins, and is active in helping them develop and promote their products. What is more, he doesn't get involved in any contract if he doesn't have a feeling for the company or confidence in its products or management. Indeed, the contracts he has turned down would probably keep most people happy for years.

Certainly he got no money for his earliest drives, as he drove under the unimaginative non-de-plume of A.N. Other to hide his racing from his mother. These early races for Jackie were impressive in that, in the hurly-burly of amateur motor racing in Scotland in those days, he drove such cars as a Porsche Super and a Marcos sportscar at a pace well beyond their apparent capabilities. He obviously had talent, and Jim Clark tried to get him to test for Colin Chapman in a Formula 3 Lotus very early in his career. However, Jackie turned down the offer, as his mother still didn't know that he was racing. It is said that she found out on the day Jackie married Helen, and a local newspaper blew the gaff on his double life as the mystery racing driver. He then spent part of his honeymoon driving his Jaguar saloon round the Nurburgring.

Once his cover had been blown, Jackie began to race regularly in Scotland with the company's E-type Jaguar demonstrator, and he had a number of wins in the car. In 1963, however, he was approached by David Murray just as his brother had been approached twelve years before, and was offered the chance of driving their Cooper Monaco sportscar and Tojeiro Buick Coupe. Recently Lord Elgin, Chairman of the Ecurie Ecosse Association, admitted that they had been at a loss to find someone who could sort out the bugs in their cars and they thought Jackie might be the man. As it transpired, Stewart gave them some of their greatest successes with both cars, even though he had his first major accident in the Cooper Monaco at Oulton Park, writing the car off.

He moved into the 1964 season determined to get more experience, and a telephone call from Charles Bridges, a Northern racing enthusiast, led to the offer of a 3.8 litre saloon Jaguar for a club relay race at Oulton. The team won the first prize. This encouraged

One of Jackie Stewart's early races was at Charterhall in 1962 where he drove a Marcos, above and above right. He also tried hill climbing with the Marcos at Rest and Be Thankful in Argyll, far right. In all his very early races he drove under the name of A. N. Other to hide the fact from his parents, but later they became reconciled with his career and his father, pictured right, was to be seen at several race meetings

Bridges, who offered to buy Jackie a full race Lotus-Cortina. But by then things had taken wing. In March 1964 Jimmy Stewart received a telephone call from Ken Tyrrell, who wanted to get Jackie down to Goodwood to try out the Formula 3 Cooper-Austin. Eventually he found him in Edinburgh. Yet before Jackie agreed to go, he telephoned three of his friends, including David Murray, to ask their advice. All told him to take the offer. He was given a full contract for Formula 3 with ten events abroad. Five days later he sat on the line at Snetterton in the pouring rain; his professional career had begun.

27

It is interesting to recall Stewart's reactions at that first race. Within three laps he was 48 seconds in the lead. Afterwards, I asked him how he had felt and he replied: 'Even to this day I don't know where the hell the rest of them got to. I don't know why they were so slow, for it wasn't as impossible as all that. There were loads of puddles and you aquaplaned at every corner, but as long as you were careful you could drive reasonably quickly.'

After he had won seven Formula 3 races in a row I asked him how it was he made it all look so easy. He answered that most young drivers in the Formula at that time didn't have the big car experience he had had, and he felt it was very important to have an apprenticeship on big powerful cars, after which the Formula 3 of that day was comparatively easy. One wonders if the same advice might be true today.

The same year, 1964, he started driving Lotus Elans for Ian Walker Racing, and was supposed to make his Le Mans debut that year

with Ninian Sanderson in an Elan, Sanderson having been a contemporary with Jimmy Stewart in the Ecurie Ecosse team. The day after Charles Bridges let Jackie out of his contract, Colin Chapman approached him in Monaco and offered a Lotus-Cortina drive with Team Lotus with Jim Clark and Peter Arundell. Within a few weeks, Jackie had made his first trip to the United States to drive a Cortina at Watkins Glen.

Drives were now being offered thick and fast: John Coombs offered him the best lightweight E-type Jaguar in the country, and an old Jaguar friend, Eric Brown, offered him a drive in his beautifully prepared XK120. He accepted both. Later he was to be seen with John Mecom, the American millionaire, who offered him a drive in his team. He drove a Formula 1 Lotus in practice at Brands Hatch, and in December had his first Formula 1 drive in South Africa, driving a Lotus.

The year had seen many changes, but these

28

changes were all planned by Stewart well in advance. In June 1964 he told me: 'If I establish myself this year as being versatile and able to drive various types of car, when it comes to next year I am going to have it clearly stuck in my mind which cars I drive best.' In 1965 he signed his first Grand Prix contract with BRM; he had made his decision.

He was seeing the world, and not all of motor racing impressed him. In 1965, for instance, following a visit to an American sportscar race at Laguna Seca, he expressed his amazement at what he had seen: 'I saw more accidents in that race than I've seen in Grand Prix and every other type of racing. It was monumental, ridiculous — they don't seem to mind bumping each other. They try to out-do each other, balk each other, and don't even look in their mirrors . . . what a carry on!' One reason for his discontent stemmed from the fact that, a week before at Riverside in California, someone in a McLaren sportscar

had deliberately thumped him on the tail on a fast corner, and he had gone spinning off into the desert.

Throughout his career Jackie Stewart has always analyzed himself. In this way he has been able to rationalize his racing so that, when he eventually became a full-time Grand Prix driver with BRM, he did less and less racing outside Grand Prix racing.

One main exception was the 1966 Indianapolis 500 race. A year earlier, Jim Clark had won the race and, with just one season in Grand Prix racing under his belt, here was Jackie Stewart in his Bowes Seal Fast Special lined up with the fastest drivers in the United States, plus Jim Clark and Graham Hill. The track was slippery, yet Stewart drove a brilliant race to trail Lloyd Ruby. Ruby's car retired around 150 laps leaving Stewart, the rookie, well in the lead. From then on there was no one else in the race. Ten laps from the end, the oil pressure faltered, then dropped, and

In 1963 Jackie Stewart was offered the chance of driving the Cooper Monaco sportscar for Ecurie Ecosse, and in 1964 he drove a 3.8 litre saloon Jaguar, below, in a club relay race at Oulton

Stewart was forced to switch off the engine and retire.

Though we have never specifically discussed that race, it would not surprise me if Stewart were to admit that it was his greatest disappointment in his racing career. The grand prize was in his lap, then he was forced to retire just ten minutes before the end of the race. A year later he went back to Indianapolis in a Lola-Ford, finished a lowly eighteenth and never competed at the circuit again.

In Grand Prix racing the portents were good. He and Jim Clark looked like sewing up this side of the sport for many years. Then in 1968 Clark was killed at Hockenheim. This accident had a profound effect on both Jackie and Helen Stewart. To understand their grief, one must understand that Jackie and Jim Clark had travelled together all over the world, and were almost inseparable friends. I was with Stewart a fortnight after Clark's accident when he had just moved to Geneva and was living in a rented flat while his house was being modified. It was obvious that Clark's death was troubling him, and he and Helen were later to admit that it was the first really 'low' period in their lives.

It helps to see Jim Clark's death in the perspective of Jackie's life at that time. When Jackie and Helen married, they lived modestly, at first in a small flat at Rhu near Helensburgh and later in a bungalow two houses away from his parents at Dumbuck. It was all very relaxed, a retreat to return to when the racing weekends were over. The first signs of Jackie's growing maturity came when he bought a beautiful turn-of-the-century house in its own grounds on top of the Hill in Helensburgh. He lavished everything on that house, and its situation denoted that he had reached the top in more ways than one. He had plans for the house, but the pace of his racing dictated that it was impossible to fly back to Glasgow every time. He needed somewhere closer to the hub of international travel.

At the same time his earnings were beginning to develop, so much so that at one time he earned more than Jim Clark. His financial advisers helped in his decision to move to Geneva, and this he did in 1968. Helen was packing the last of her things to leave Helens-

burgh the day Jim Clark was killed: on the day the Stewarts had severed their direct connections with the area where they were born and brought up, their lives had been hit by the first of many tragedies in motor racing.

Later, of course, they were to lose other close friends such as Jochen Rindt, Piers Courage, Gerry Birrell and François Cevert, and there is no doubting the effect these deaths had on them both. Helen saw Grand Prix racing in the later years very much as a job of work which had to be done, with less of the fun and emotion that one feels when with close friends.

For Jackie, motor racing was still something more than a job and, watching him in the years from 1968 until his retirement, one could see a true master perfecting his craft. He was undoubtedly the best driver of his age, with a command of his sport which was amazing to watch. To my mind, one memory of Jackie Stewart will always remain. The race was the British Grand Prix of 1971 at Silverstone, just another Grand Prix for Stewart but one in which I wanted to try to appreciate his technique.

I was able to select a spot on the outside of Woodcote corner where the best drivers come round in a long drift at about 130 mph. I squatted down until my eye-line was level with that of the drivers and then watched. At that speed even the smallest ripple on the track has its effect on a racing car, and Stewart came round with the car twitching fractionally from side to side as he read the bumps. It was the finest display of Grand Prix driving I have ever seen, and how a man could control a car at that speed is something I shall never know.

Only later in a conversation did Jackie admit that in his last two seasons he felt he had gone to the absolute limit of his car, his tyres and himself. He had given of himself fully, and he realized that when driving at this pitch one mistake would have meant disaster. There was no way he was going to spin and survive; he would fly right off the road and hit the first thing that got in his way. That he didn't, and that in his entire career he only had one bad accident, shows that from time to time there emerges a sportsman who is head and shoulders above everyone else.

Make-up of a winning car

Eric Dymock, Motor Racing Correspondent of the *Guardian* and co-author of a book with Stewart, traces the development of 003, the car that became unique in motor- racing history

Some racing cars never reach the start line. Others perform indifferently and never finish. Some do better and may even aspire to winning. Cars that win a Grand Prix or two before being damaged, or retired, or overtaken technically by their rivals, are rare. A car that survives seventeen Grand Prix races, wins eight of them and carries its driver to a world championship is not only exceptional — in modern Grand Prix racing history it is unique.

In 1970 Ken Tyrrell, who had discovered the talents of Jackie Stewart and had brought him into single seater racing in 1964, found himself without a competitive Formula 1 racing car. Stewart had won the world championship in 1969 driving a French Matra-Ford. The car had been managed by Tyrrell and run from his

tiny timber-yard in the middle of a Surrey wood. It was an unlikely place from which to offer a challenge to the world but with Matra, the French missile firm's expertise, and the power of the Ford-Cosworth V8 engine — designed by Keith Duckworth and built in Northampton — the team carried all before it. Success, however, was to bring its own problems.

For in 1970 Matra was associated with Chrysler, and this prevented them supplying Tyrrell with cars to run using Ford engines. International business politics intruded on to the Grand Prix track, and Tyrrell had to look elsewhere for his cars. Matra were keen Stewart should run a car with their own V12 engine, but Stewart himself felt it would never be a match for the Ford-Cosworth, and he

The 1971 Spanish Grand Prix, below left, was the
breakthrough for 003 — its first Grand Prix win. In its
next race, the International Trophy at Silverstone, the
003 suffered a serious setback when Jackie Stewart
crashed spectacularly, leaving only a week for it to be
repaired before the Monaco Grand Prix. In the event,
however, it was ready, and Jackie Stewart rewarded
the hard-working mechanics with a copybook
performance, leading the race from start to finish, below

STEWART

turned out to be right. Matra ran their own team instead and never won a world championship race. But it still left Stewart without a car for 1970, and buying one was not to prove easy.

None of the established teams would sell him one. Lotus, Ferrari, McLaren and BRM all felt, not without cause, that a car driven by Jackie Stewart would present too much of a threat. They risked being beaten by one of their own designs. Only one firm had nothing to lose, the newly-formed March Engineering, to whom the prestige of having the world champion at the wheel meant more than having their own drivers overtaken.

So Tyrrell began 1970 with the March-Ford, which at least kept the team going. He was providing Stewart with wheels and keeping him under contract until something better turned up. Tyrrell had no idea at first what it would be, but he decided after a while that, after years of running other people's cars, he would have to build a new car himself.

The first step was to engage a designer and the choice fell on an engineer associated with the Matra MS84, the four-wheel drive car the team had already used experimentally. Derek Gardner had worked with Harry Ferguson Research, the transmission specialists, and had earned a reputation as a gifted engineer. But he had never designed a racing car in his life.

Two of the predecessors of the Tyrrell were the Matra-Ford, pictured above left during the 1969 German Grand Prix and the March-Ford pictured far left inset during the 1970 Race of Champions at Brands Hatch. 1971 saw the arrival of the Tyrrell-Ford 003 and Ken Tyrrell, pictured left with Jackie Stewart, was suitably rewarded with eight Grand Prix wins, one of which was the 1971 British Grand Prix, opposite, at Silverstone

Stewart was not the only one at Tyrrell Racing with talent, however. Ken Tyrrell has a gift for organization, thoroughness and picking the right people for the job. In the spring of 1970, and in the strictest secrecy, Gardner began designing a racing car that was to make the most dramatic Grand Prix debut ever. That summer, working in Ken Tyrrell's timber-yard and behind closed doors, the Tyrrell team carefully put together a car that would win the world championship at its first attempt.

In the motor racing world that autumn the news of the Tyrrell was a sensation. Tyrrell-Ford 001 appeared in the non-championship Oulton Park Gold Cup meeting and set a new lap record before retiring with engine trouble. At Monza, in the Italian Grand Prix the following weekend, Stewart drove the car in practice, but raced the March instead. He was in no mood for motor racing. His friend, Jochen Rindt, had died in a Lotus during practice, making it no time to try out a new racing car.

It was not until the Canadian Grand Prix that the Tyrrell made its world championship debut. Stewart had trouble in practice when the throttle slides stuck, and on the second day a rear wheel nut worked loose. It looked as though the race was going to be a walk-over for Ferrari but, only moments before practice ended, Stewart took 001 out and snatched the pole position with the fastest practice lap. It was decided. This time the March remained in the garage and the Tyrrell would race in a Grand Prix for the first time.

Stewart led for 32 astonishing laps of the bumpy St Jovite track, pulling away from the opposition all the time. Then a stub axle broke and he was lucky not to crash. The car was out of the race but it hardly mattered. Tyrrell and Stewart could see that their shy, quietly-spoken designer had made them a car that was a match for anything in the world. The next race was another triumph, when Stewart led for 82 of the 108 laps of the United States Grand Prix at Watkins Glen, before an oil pipe broke and once again he had to retire.

The prospects for the New Year of 1971 looked good. Two replicas of 001 were laid down. The design had been proved and Tyrrell was confident. Stewart's position as the fastest driver in the world was beyond dispute, and he knew he had a good car. Of course it had to be developed: the successors to 001 were to be constructed even more carefully. The monocoque hull, of aluminium panels rivetted together to form a strong bath-tub containing the fuel tanks and the driver, was filed and fitted together by hand. There was nothing very revolutionary about the design. Its conception and layout were not unlike any of its rivals, but Gardner's brief had been to build a car that would be strong. It had to take the abuse of a season's racing without needing patchwork maintenance. It had to be easy to work on, so that routine jobs between races would be easy; engine and gearbox replacements could be carried out with the minimum of delay and the maximum of efficiency. Tyrrell's years in racing had taught him that, in the heat of a tear-down and rebuild at the track, if something could be put together wrongly sooner or later it probably would. The car was designed to suit. He knew also that a driver worked best when his car was reliable and strong enough not to shatter in an accident.

The Tyrrell's strength was soon tested. During the South African Grand Prix, the first race of the 1971 season, the team's number two driver, the young Frenchman, François Cevert, blinded by sweat in the torrid heat of the Johannesburg summer, crashed heavily. The first of the replicas, Tyrrell-Ford 002, was a write-off in its first race. But Stewart, still driving 001, came second to Mario Andretti's Ferrari. In the non-championship Questor Grand Prix, at which a new American track was used for the first time, 001 was second again, and second once more in the Race of Champions at Brands Hatch.

The next round of the world championship was the Grand Prix of Spain on the 3.25 mile, twisting track in Barcelona's Montjuich Park, a demanding circuit in the middle of the city, and the second replica, chassis number 003, was ready. It looked the same, in brilliant blue, with its high front aerofoil extending across the front of the car, with the air intake underneath. Like most of its rivals, it used the three-litre Ford-Cosworth DFV engine, producing about 440 bhp, at 10,000 rpm, about

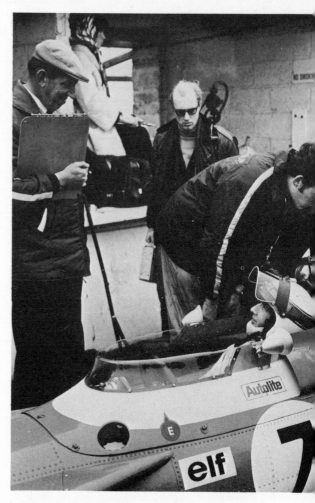

Team Tyrrell progressed from the Matra-Ford, above, in 1969, to the March-Ford, top right, in 1970, through to the Tyrrell-Ford 001, above right, at the end of 1970

ten times the power of one family saloon but in a car weighing rather less. It used Lucas fuel injection and Lucas transistorized ignition, Ford-Motorcraft spark plugs, and fuel and oil supplied by the French Elf petrol company, the team's major sponsor. The FPT fuel cells stored 42 gallons inside the rounded hull. Fuel consumption was $5-6\frac{1}{2}$ mpg and, although lower geared for acceleration on the hairpins and short straights of Montjuich, with a high final drive ratio, 003's top speed would be not far short of 200 mph.

The Spanish Grand Prix on 18 April 1971 was the breakthrough — the first Grand Prix win for 003. Stewart made the second row of the starting grid behind the Ferraris of Ickx

car, with breathtaking precision, straight at the television camera and it seemed that only the stout earth bank prevented 003 from plunging straight into a million living-rooms.

It was a serious setback. The Monaco Grand Prix was only a week away, and 003 had had a corner knocked off. That precious monocoque, built with such painstaking thoroughness only weeks before, had to be unpicked and put right in a matter of days. True, 004 was now complete, but 003 was well-tried and proven. This was the car Stewart wanted to use.

In the event, it was ready, and Stewart rewarded the hard-working Roger Hill, his joint chief mechanic ever since he had driven for Tyrrell, with one of his copybook performances. He set the fastest lap in practice, led the race from start to finish, and took the lap record to 88.58 mph. With two wins and one second, he was well on the way to a world title.

At Zandvoort it rained. The Dutch Grand Prix is held on the coast, and a drenching wind off the North Sea blew across the dunes, coating the track with a damp, sandy paste. A fault in 003's handling was traced to the brakes, causing the rear wheels to grab after the pedal was released. None of the Goodyear runners did well and Stewart finished eleventh, five laps behind the leaders Jacky Ickx (Ferrari) and Pedro ·Rodriguez (BRM). It was a wet watershed for Ickx. Throughout the remainder of the year he finished in only one more race.

The French Grand Prix was on the new Paul Ricard track, a world away from wet, windy Holland. In Mediterranean sunshine, the opposition melted away. In every practice session Stewart was fastest. He led the race from start to finish. On lap two he set a new circuit record, and, as though to underline his success, François Cevert took second place at half distance and held it till the end.

The opposition was furious. Tyrrell must be cheating. Officials even had to check 003's fuel because the Tyrrell engines *sounded* different. Samples were taken and of course its fuel was just the same as everyone else's. But certainly, the cars *were* faster on the straights than even the twelve-cylinder Ferraris, which was unexpected. And they *did* sound different

and Regazzoni and Chris Amon's Matra-Simca V12. Ickx went into the lead with Stewart behind him, but remained in front for only five laps. Stewart overtook and almost at once pulled out ten seconds with a display of masterly driving that had the Spanish crowd gasping. It was the first win for the Tyrrell, the first for a Ford-Cosworth-engined car since the previous October, Goodyear's first win for over a year, and Stewart's third Spanish Grand Prix in a row. Ickx's only compensation was the lap record at 99.64 mph.

The team's euphoria did not last long. In the International Trophy at Silverstone, 003 crashed. The race, which did not count for the championship, was in two heats and, after winning the first, 003's throttle stuck open on the first corner of the first lap of the second heat. Stewart thundered straight on into one of the best publicized crashes ever. He aimed the

from all the other Cosworths. Tyrrell pointed to the air scoop above the engines. It had been fitted at Zandvoort but showed no advantage on the rain-soaked track. Here at Ricard it was different.

Derek Gardner had reasoned that the air round the inlet trumpets of the engine must be turbulent, and ought to be cleaned up. 'It is like blindfolding a man in a pub,' he says. 'He will drink the froth off his pint first.' Removing the froth from the slipstream allowed the engine to breathe more easily, and ensured that it delivered the same 440 horse-power as it did on the test bed. Nearly every other Grand Prix team copied the idea within the month. Another aerodynamic development in the Tyrrell was a rounded nose cone which improved the handling. The broad front wing was exerting too much downforce out near the wheels, making it too sensitive at high speed.

In the British Grand Prix at Silverstone, Jackie Stewart and 003 made it four victories in five races — despite a last-minute drama. While the engine was being warmed up 50 minutes before the start, the mechanics discovered the oil scavenge pump had failed because a tiny set-screw was missing. Replacement was not normally possible without removing the engine. But the mechanics squirmed round it, put the screw back, guessed at its correct torque setting, and received their reward a little over an hour and a half later when Stewart not only won, having led from lap 4 to lap 68, but pushed the lap record up to 131.88 mph.

In the German Grand Prix on the remodelled Nurburgring, the twisting four-teen-mile track in the Eifel Mountains with over 170 corners and rated as the most testing track for drivers in the world, Stewart led from the second corner to the finish. Cevert came second and scored the fastest lap. Nothing, it seemed, could interrupt the progress of the Tyrrell twins.

Austria the same month looked like deciding the world championship. It had never been concluded so early in the season before but no one had ever had a season like this. Stewart's domination of every race was total. And in Austria he did decide the championship, but

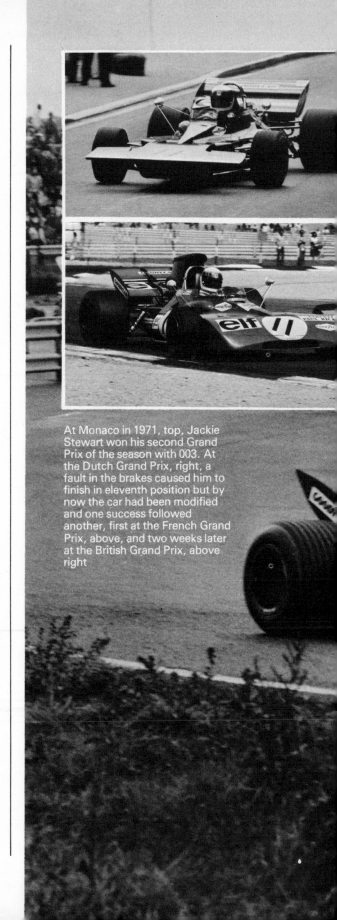

At Monaco in 1971, top, Jackie Stewart won his second Grand Prix of the season with 003. At the Dutch Grand Prix, right, a fault in the brakes caused him to finish in eleventh position but by now the car had been modified and one success followed another, first at the French Grand Prix, above, and two weeks later at the British Grand Prix, above right

not as he wanted. In 1969 Stewart took the title in a dramatic dash out of the last corner at Monza, wheel to wheel with his great rival Rindt. In 1971 he gained it sitting in the pits, having walked back after his left rear stub axle had broken and the car had slithered to a halt in a shower of sparks. Of his main rivals for the title, Ickx was already out with electrical trouble, and Peterson well back. Stewart had been lying third.

The next race for the champion-elect was Monza, where 003 again failed to finish, this time owing to engine trouble. Ken Tyrrell has nine Cosworth DFVs, which allows some in for overhaul while others are in the field. Each engine is rebuilt after a race, and 003 would probably mount each of the nine at one time or other. Gearboxes are rebuilt and suspension arms renewed, like aircraft components after a certain 'fatigue life'. Brake discs are changed (003's entire braking system was chopped and changed a number of times), and the nose piece and the rear wing are also redeveloped. Only the hull remained the same throughout its life and that was repaired twice.

Canada once again was wet for the Grand Prix, but what a difference from Zandvoort, earlier in the year! It was Stewart's sixth win of the season. He used a new Goodyear wet weather tyre specially developed to avenge Zandvoort, where the first eight finishers were on Firestone. The race was stopped owing to rain and bad light after four-fifths of the distance had been run.

In America, at Watkins Glen in upstate New York. François Cevert's dream came true; he won his first Grand Prix. Tragically, it was on the track where he was to lose his life two years later. Stewart led until his tyres overheated, and he dropped to fifth. But the destination of the 1971 world championship of drivers as well as the Constructors' Cup was secure. Stewart's total of victories was short of the late Jim Clark's seven in his first championship year of 1963 but, in the context of the closeness of the competition and the demanding nature of the season's programme, the achievement was at least equal to Clark's.

The secret lay largely in 003's reliability. If Ickx had finished more races, for example, he might have offered a stronger challenge.

Ronnie Peterson (March-Ford), who finished second in the championship, was more of a threat to Stewart, finishing four races in second place. François Cevert finished the season third in the championship, emphasizing how correct Tyrrell's brief to Gardner had been, that he wanted a strong car, and also a reliable one. The designer was already at work on something more sophisticated, but 003 had proved its worth even if it never raced again.

Yet there was no pressure on Tyrrell to change the car. It was successful, and for 1972 it looked as though it would remain so. The car was the same even down to the advertising stickers on the sides for the first race, the Argentina Grand Prix at the Autodromo Aimirante Brown in Buenos Aires. Many of 003's rivals were already new designs, but Stewart lost pole position on the grid only after an outstanding effort by Carlos Reutemann,

In the 1971 German Grand Prix Jackie Stewart led from the second corner to the finish. His team mate, François Cevert, came second and scored the fastest lap

anxious to prove to his fellow countrymen that he was a match for anyone.

In the race Stewart led from start to finish half a minute ahead of anyone else. Cevert ran fourth until an oil line to the gearbox came off and the box seized up. This was a disappointment, but otherwise it looked as though 1971 was repeating itself and successes would follow to order. It was only January; but Stewart was to wait till July before he took the chequered flag again.

In South Africa and under a hot sun it still looked set fair for the Tyrrells. Stewart set the fastest lap ever of the Kyalami track during tyre testing before the race, and best times on each of the three practice days. He had a little trouble when the rear wing collapsed at speed after a pin fell out of a support, but came to the start line looking every inch a winner. He took the lead on lap two, fought off a strong challenge from Mike Hailwood, but after 45 of the race's 79 laps 003's gearbox seized.

At Jarama, the Spanish track near Madrid, the Tyrrells were in some disarray. Stewart tried the new 004 and tyres of different compounds in a desperate effort to get on to the front row of the starting grid. He made a good start in the race, taking the lead on lap five but, instead of the usual runaway victory, began to fall back. Fittipaldi took over the lead on lap nine and Ickx pushed him back to third six laps later. He remained out of contention until near the end of the race when, astonishingly, he spun, damaging the front of the car. Clearly, something was wrong with either the world champion or his car. In fact, it was the driver who was off-colour. Stewart was feeling the first effects of the ulcer that would virtually lose him the 1972 World Championship.

43

At Monaco it rained, and Jean-Pierre Beltoise scored his first and only Grand Prix win for BRM. Stewart splashed his way round in 004 to fourth place, and announced later he would not be racing again until he had dealt with his ulcer. This meant he missed Belgium, where Cevert was second, and did not race again until the French Grand Prix.

Stewart's return was a triumph. The race on the difficult Clermont-Ferrand circuit, plunging through the Auvergne Mountains, looked like being Chris Amon's first world championship win in nine years, until he was stopped half-way by a puncture. Instead, Stewart took 003 to its final win. The Clermont track was notorious for loose stones causing punctures. Stewart kept clear of the rough kerbs and gravel and was almost the only leading car to escape tyre trouble.

But time was running out for the veteran car. Gardner's new design 005 had been announced, and duly crashed by Cevert in practice at Clermont before Stewart had had a chance to drive it. But Cevert had shown how fast it was, and it was now only a matter of the time taken up with its final developments before it would take 003's place as the team's flagship.

Stewart delayed 005's arrival by crashing it at Brands Hatch in practice for the British Grand Prix. So 003 was pressed into service once again. But Emerson Fittipaldi, driving the John Player Special, had the bit between his teeth. He had won Spain and Belgium, taking advantage of Stewart's loss of form, and showed no sign of giving up his advantage. Stewart got to within a second of him at Brands but never managed to overtake. At the Nurburgring it was Ickx who won for Ferrari, and 003's last race. Stewart battled from fifth place to challenge Clay Regazzoni for second, an uphill job in an eighteen-month-old car against the best and latest in Grand Prix racing. As he came up to overtake, Regazzoni challenged him for the next corner, the cars touched and Stewart hit the guard rail. It was the end of the road for 003.

The monocoque was repaired but the car never raced again. Chassis 005 came out in time to win Stewart the last two races of the season, but too late to wrest the championship from Fittipaldi. Tyrrell 003 went into honourable retirement as one of the most successful Grand Prix cars ever, and certainly the most successful of modern times. It was exhibited throughout the world before being presented to Jackie Stewart at a dinner given by Ford in the Savoy Hotel, London, in December 1973 to mark his retirement from motor racing.

Ken Tyrrell said that the first time Stewart drove the car he did not like it, but admitted later that Stewart did not seem to like any car much first time out. He said 003 was as near identical to 002 and 004 as could be, but this was the car that had won the races. Stewart has described it as 'a well-principled sort of car', with its worst fault being its indifferent behaviour on bumpy tracks. He blames its crashes in Spain and Silverstone on sticking throttle slides, but it was a car that never gave its mechanics trouble, and must have more than earned its keep for Team Tyrrell.

The Canadian Grand Prix in September 1971 gave Jackie Stewart his sixth win of the season and ensured him the World Championship, right. In July 1972 Stewart took 003 to its final win in the French Grand Prix, below

An estimate of the man

Hugh McIlvanney, one of Scotland's leading sportswriters, takes a look at Jackie Stewart the racing driver, a man anaesthetized against the terrible possibilities, hooked on the marvellous, irreplaceable excitement

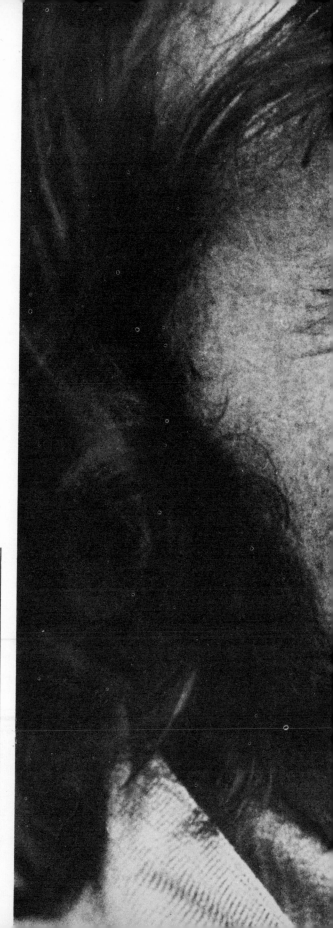

When all the rationalizing has been done and the equations are neatly resolved, there is always the mystery of the animal in the machine. There is one half of Jackie Stewart's nature that would encourage the wild fallacy that he is a computer thinly disguised as a man. The suggestion has been made in print and he has chosen to recognize it not as the profound insult it is but as a tribute he longs hopelessly to justify.

This response comes from the part of him that has an almost religious belief in self-control, in ensuring that mind and will have the maximum effect on personal destiny, the part of him that plays the percentages in nearly all areas of his life with such relentless calculation. But he has too much intelligence and too great an appetite for self-examination to be unaware that there is a second Jackie Stewart, one who has gone, in his own phrase,

'to the edge of experience' and come back without a visible scar because of an animal vigour and a subtlety of reaction well beyond the scope of any computer ever devized.

The technical, analytical man has always had a co-driver whose senses were heightened in crisis to a degree that few human beings can ever know, whose instinctive perceptions were as a flood to the ordinary mortal's trickle. Those Formula 1 cars that roared in Stewart's hands to 27 Grand Prix victories and three world championships were running, ultimately, not on petrol but on blood, and their real controls were the nerve-ends of a man.

It is hard for the rest of us to comprehend how remarkable in his case those nerve-ends are. For a start, he takes in through his eyes far more than can ever be explained by the mere fact of possessing 20/20 vision or having had such a prolonged exposure to dramatic situations. When he is driving at speed he seems able to see in slow-motion, to feed his brain so many 'frames' of the most fleeting occurrence that it can absorb the details almost at leisure.

'It is not the efficiency of the eyesight that is important,' he says. 'It is the consumption of vision, how much you assimilate. I remember seeing a hare running up the track towards my car once and plotting its course. I saw it long before I needed to see it and, by the time I closed on it at 200 mph, I had worked out all the possible consequences of that hare's behaviour. I knew just what it could provide in the way of trouble. Some people have great eyes but they have tunnel vision. My eyes cover a tremendously wide field. I have what is some-times called peripheral vision. If there were doubtful weather conditions when we were racing, I would literally see the first person move for shelter, just about see the first to hunch his shoulders against the coming rain, certainly the very first flourish of an umbrella, regardless of how fast I was going.'

On his own evidence, his hearing, too, would appear to function abnormally.

'If somebody dropped a five-gallon drum behind me without warning I wouldn't be likely to jump, unless I was very tired and my responses were blunted. Noises that startle most people somehow seem less sudden and therefore less frightening to me.'

The impression he conveys is that abrupt sounds enter his consciousness as a flow rather than as explosions. This phenomenon need not indicate that he has extraordinarily fine hearing, such as a musician might have, but rather that there is accelerated communica-tion between his senses and the part of his brain that dictates the appropriate reaction. It's a handy commodity to have, especially if you are earning your living in the deadliest sport civilized man has ever practised.

The duality in his nature is something Stewart has never found difficult to recognize.

'If you look at my face, you will see that one half of it is completely different from the other,' he tells you. 'It's not hard to guess that I'm a Gemini.'

On one side he identifies his lighter, more adventurous self, 'the competitor in me, the tiger.' The other, he thinks, reflects a heavier, more conservative character, the unyielding campaigner for greater safety and social re-sponsibility in motor racing.

Such fine distinctions could occur only to the individual who has shaving-mirror familiarity with a set of features, but anyone who has seen Stewart even briefly will confirm that the face is strange and arresting. At times, when the eyelids droop above the long nose and the mouth tightens, it is as austere as that of a Medici pope. There are occasions, how-ever, when it is enlivened by a strictly twentieth-century worldliness, when it is about as papal as his corduroy cap. In such moments his use of words is liable to be cool, vivid and bitingly selective, with a wit that remains es-sentially west of Scotland, in spite of the distance he has put between himself and his social and geographical beginnings.

Even his driving, he acknowledges, has always been in some respects peculiarly Scottish. He feels it is no coincidence that from 1962 until 1973 the world of motor racing was dominated by two men from a tiny nation of five million people, first by Jim Clark and then by himself. Clearly, he says, the Scots are especially well equipped by breeding, temperament and tradition to cope with the unique demands of the modern Grand Prix

Jackie Stewart feels it is no coincidence that from 1962 until 1973 the world of motor racing was dominated by two men from a tiny nation of five million people, first by Jim Clark and then by himself

circuit.

'As a race we are extremely determined, but we are also canny. Ours is not a blind determination. We are very much aware of what is going on and we are able to direct the resolution in our natures into the right channels — to make it effective. It goes without saying that that other kind of determination, the kind that is not informed by intelligence and awareness, can lead you into a lot of dark alleys. And in driving it can lead you into the darkest alley of all, the last one.

'Jimmy Clark never had a trace of that weakness. The reasons for his death are not to be found in any flaw in his driving. Jimmy and I drove in very much the same way, smoothly and cleanly and with economy. With us there were no elbows and arms flailing around in the wind. We were precise and unspectacular — rather conservative, in fact.' What he means is that the only spectacular thing about them was their speed. They were the fastest conservatives on four wheels.

A seam of understatement runs through everything Stewart says about his career and through the attitudes that shaped it. His assessment of the importance of bravery in the make-up of an outstanding driver is heavy with qualifications, with the sort of reservations that would scarcely be acceptable if they did not come from a man who, season after season, found himself able to step from the gravesides of his close friends back on to the grid that had launched them to oblivion. He admits that such behaviour would come within most definitions of bravery, but he is ambivalent about how much credit is due to the man who acts that way.

'I have never considered courage a vital ingredient in my business,' he insists. 'I see most courageous men as being fools. One instance in which I would question the popular conception of heroism is the rescue attempt after a bad crash on the track. To me, the crucial thing there is the ability to take the most relevant and the most effective action when confronted with, say, a blazing car. There must be instant analysis of the situation and then immediate but logical action. The man who dives into the flames, without really knowing what he's about, is doing no service to

49

the trapped driver. Whatever the risks he is taking, he may be just wasting time.

'Of course, there is the other question of what it takes to continue after someone you know well has been killed on the track. When that happens and you, by your own choice, go back out and go on doing precisely that thing that wiped out your friend, well I suppose this could be said to be a form of courage. It is difficult to explain to your loved ones why you want to go on. Sometimes you need courage to do that. But there is great selfishness, too. The whole experience is weird.

'First you see the destruction of a car and a man's body. Then you see the hopeless tearing of the heart in his wife and family and the way they are invaded by despondency about their future. You see how your family view what is happening and how bad it is for them and yet you go out and do it again. Confronted by their case, you accept that motor racing is totally futile and stupid and still you carry on. You are able to do it because what is out there is so exhilarating for the selfish man behind the wheel. It is as if someone has given you an injection that anaesthetizes you against the terrible possibilities and leaves you hooked on the marvellous, irreplaceable excitement.'

In that last sentence it is the voice of the tiger we are hearing once again and it surely drowns all talk of computerized driving, all the allegations that Stewart has made racing a soul-less, cold-blooded science.

'There are those who have said I removed the romance from the game, that with me as champion it was no longer the swashbuckling spectacular it had been. When I campaigned for more realistic safety measures, these people said I had no guts. Well, I have the track record to answer that. And, as far as the first accusation is concerned the majority of the public don't seem to have found me a dull champion.'

Any suggestion that they have would be hard to reconcile with his income or with the reception given all over the world to the slight, long-haired figure who moves with a briskness that suggests every moment has a Le Mans start. His millions of admirers long ago endorsed his belief that a racing driver has no obligation to get himself maimed or oblitera-

ted. They know that anyone who claims that a man could win 27 Grands Prix while driving scared is certifiable.

In his crusade for greater safety on the tracks they see the desire of a courageous and brilliant driver to eradicate gratuitous hazards and so avoid unnecessary, pointless loss of life. He is doubly entitled to be heard. The first justification is that he has seen so many of his close friends cut down in their vibrant prime. The second is simply that he was a winner, not a loser, and therefore can never be accused of whining. There was an occasion when Arnold Palmer, having spreadeagled the world's best golfers in the British Open at Troon, came off and criticized the course. He was speaking from unassailable strength. So is Stewart. 'They have a great problem with me because I have done it,' he says. 'Anybody who hadn't done it would have no one's ears.'

The Belgian Grand Prix at Zolder in 1973 was a perfect demonstration of how he provided his own armament in the safety con-

Jackie Stewart leads Clay Regazzoni in the 1973
Belgian Grand Prix, a race he had tried to stop because
of the bad condition of the track

troversy. Part of the track began to break up in practice and drivers, led by Stewart, demanded that the track owners should put matters right or call off the race. Finally, the owners agreed that, if the track did not hold up on the last practice, they would cancel the event. It did hold up, though only just.

On the day, seven cars crashed at the one corner that had caused most of the trouble, a place where, as Stewart recalls, 'there were only two grooves of track a few inches wide that were safe — the rest was like marbles.' The crusader in him was still angered by the conditions. But the competitor in him won the race anyway.

Now there will be no more Grand Prix battles for him but he will be competing in one way or another as long as he lives. Anyone who saw him in the recent televised athletic contest for superstars of British sport will know he has the kind of heart that could be classified as a deadly weapon. Defeat is as alien to him as the ocean bed is to a hawk, and whoever takes him

on at anything must be ready to come second. He will have more time now to show the skill with a gun that made him a world-class clay pigeon shot before he turned to driving. As the grandson of a gamekeeper, he is also a keen fisherman and he hopes to improve his golf and his tennis, though not at the expense of his wife and children who now look forward to having him instead of fear for company. Deprivation they will never know, for he is sure to remain the least complacent of the big earners.

'Where are you?' he was asking someone on the telephone when I left him. 'Glasgow? Well, you deserve each other.' The same can be said about Jackie Stewart and success.

Jackie Stewart the family man

Now that the Grand Prix battles are over, Jackie Stewart looks forward to spending more time with the family he loves and to catching up on some of the moments he has missed in his children's development

Sometimes the pressures became too great for the children, and Paul, the older of the two boys, suggested that, if his father wanted to earn pennies and still go on driving, he was sure he could get a job driving the school bus. Now they can relax, knowing that at last their father is safe, and enjoy life together at their home in Switzerland

The success behind Team Tyrrell

Stuart Turner, Ford's Director of Motor Sport and Manager of their Advanced Vehicle Operations, shows how single-mindedness, dedication and organization ensured Ken Tyrrell's success in building the car and the team

To win consistently in international motor sport, especially in the dizzy heights of Formula 1, you need three ingredients: a driver, a car and an organization. The secret behind Team Tyrrell's success is that all three aspects have been properly covered, largely due to Ken Tyrrell's single-minded application to the sport. His talent for spotting the best drivers of the day is legendary and needs no further amplification from me. He is pretty good at sizing up cars and engines too: he placed his order for three Formula 1 Ford-Cosworth Grand Prix engines at eight o'clock on the morning after the unit had won its first race in its first appearance.

It is the third leg of the tripod for success in which Ken Tyrrell really excels — organization. Tyrrell himself says that he spends his working life concentrating on just one thing — how to win Formula 1 races. When he's not actually involved in masterminding the Team's next outing, he will sit and think, and then think some more, about how he can produce better results than those of his rivals. Apart from plain hard work, it is this dedication that is the key to the Team's success.

Tyrrell says: 'It's important not to get distracted at all. McLaren have been involved in Formula 2, CanAm, Indianapolis American-style racing and Formula 1, all at the same time. Colin Chapman is involved in any number of projects, including how to run a motor car business, as well as organizing and designing the John Player Specials. I have the time to think about silly things, and it's often those silly things that let my opponents down.' Carrying the comparison to its conclusion, Ken adds, with a disarming grin: 'If Colin Chapman gave everything up to do Formula 1 seven days a week, he'd be absolutely unbeatable . . . thank God he is much too busy to do that.'

I particularly remember Ken and John Cooper attending some of our full-scale test days during my spell as Competitions Manager at BMC. Both would attend as talent spotters, and I have always thought that Tyrrell first

Jackie Stewart leads the field in a Tyrrell-Ford 006, far left, near the start of the 1973 German Grand Prix. Above, he drives a BRM in the 1965 British Grand Prix at Silverstone

spotted Jackie Stewart when he was busy lopping a second lap from each of our star drivers — using their regular cars! However, the employment of J. Y. Stewart as a regular racing driver for Mr K. Tyrrell, proud owner of the Surrey timber merchants of that name and himself a former driver of competence (Ken vigorously denies any talent in the hot seat, but he wasn't *that* bad), comes some way through the development of Ken Tyrrell's role as an entrant/constructor.

The basis of today's Team Tyrrell took shape in 1960. It was that year that Tyrrell first ran cars for a new Formula for the 1960 season — Formula Junior. The sporting potential of the Mini had interested BMC in motor racing, and John Cooper — the originator of the Mini-Cooper that used a lot of engine know-how acquired from F/Junior — asked Ken Tyrrell if he would run a couple of single seaters with factory-loaned BMC engines. Tyrrell hired a pair of mechanics, and those two men are still with him today. Alan Stait is now a foreman machinist and Neil Davis is the present works manager.

Despite the success that was to come his way in the next eight years up to the beginning of 1968, Tyrrell remained a part-time entrant, splitting his effort between the family timber business and racing. However, as the racing cars were based at the wood-yard, this meant that Tyrrell did not have to break that famous concentration too often.

From 1960 to 1964 Tyrrell ran the factory Coopers with success. Drivers who passed under the gimlet eye and hatchet Tyrrell profile, and who then went on into the snug Cooper seats, included Henry Taylor and John Surtees. Taylor scored a win that Ken still remembers at the all-important supporting event to the Monaco Grand Prix and was to graduate to Formula 1.

When Taylor retired from motor sport (he also rallied extensively in works Fords through the mid-60s) he joined Ford at Boreham as Competitions Manager, and had a strong hand in the establishment of Ford Advanced Vehicle Operations. In short, his was the kind of success that Tyrrell enjoys spotting. Team-mate Surtees progressed to the point of taking the World Formula 1 Championship for Ferrari,

adding to the trophies he had already collected when he dominated World Championship motor cycle racing. Ken particularly remembers Surtees's outstanding first race for his team, when he managed a resounding second overall to Jim Clark at Goodwood.

The big break for Tyrrell came in his final year with Cooper-BMC machinery. Warwick Banks was signed and proved an excellent all-round driver, but Tyrrell had heard about a young Scotsman who was doing remarkable things with Jaguar sportscars. John Young Stewart presented himself at Goodwood for a test day that has passed into motor-racing history, with Jackie astonishing Ken, John Cooper and Bruce McLaren.

Come 1964, the Tyrrell-Cooper-Stewart combination provided some astounding re-

sults. In cold statistics JYS won fourteen of the sixteen races for which Ken entered him. In the fifteenth his clutch broke on the startline and he had to settle for second, while in the sixteenth event he was a non-starter. Ken was full of praise for the smooth and astoundingly fast style of his new driver after that Goodwood test day, but never more so than with his performance in his very first race for Ken. It was wet and windy, as if often is at Norfolk's Snetterton track but this hardly deterred Stewart, who, within the first lap, pulled out no less than twelve seconds on the top quality opposition.

Many will not know that Tyrrell also operated a racing saloon car team for Cooper with equal success. In 1963 John Love took the British title in a Tyrrell Mini-Cooper, while in

1964 Warwick Banks took one to a win in the European Touring Championship.

Ken showed true team manager initiative in these European events, even to the extent of taking along a complete class of cars for one qualifying round to ensure that the result was positively certain. In fact, the European title wasn't decided until the very last lap of the last race at Monza when, after a race-long battle of wits with Alan Mann's Ford team, the class-leading Anglia ran out of fuel and gave Ken's team the title.

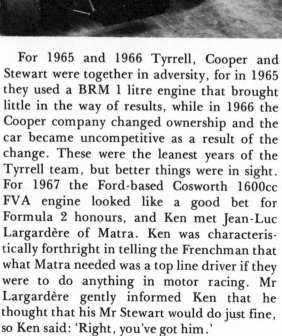

For 1965 and 1966 Tyrrell, Cooper and Stewart were together in adversity, for in 1965 they used a BRM 1 litre engine that brought little in the way of results, while in 1966 the Cooper company changed ownership and the car became uncompetitive as a result of the change. These were the leanest years of the Tyrrell team, but better things were in sight. For 1967 the Ford-based Cosworth 1600cc FVA engine looked like a good bet for Formula 2 honours, and Ken met Jean-Luc Largardère of Matra. Ken was characteristically forthright in telling the Frenchman that what Matra needed was a top line driver if they were to do anything in motor racing. Mr Largardère gently informed Ken that he thought that his Mr Stewart would do just fine, so Ken said: 'Right, you've got him.'

Tyrrell then had to persuade Jackie that Goodwood was the place to be on a cold October day, when the Matra could be tested as a Formula 3 chassis with BRM power. Jackie was inclined to think it was all some sort of Gallic joke . . . until he tried the car. He realized what a beautiful chassis it had, an opinion that was reinforced for Ken when he went over to inspect the French factory and saw that Matra's experience in the aerospace industry was proving just as useful in car construction.

Under the Tyrrell Racing Organization entry Ken hired Jacky Ickx, originally to cover Formula 3, but the Belgian's talent very swiftly took him into a second Matra-Ford FVA alongside Stewart. This was a great year in Formula 2 for the green Tyrrell-entered

In the summer of 1970, working in Ken Tyrrell's timber-yard, the team put together a car that was to cause a sensation

Matras, because Jacky Ickx took the 1967 European Championship Drivers' Title in one of their cars, and added further to the Tyrrell reputation for talent spotting with some exceptional drives.

Quite why Ken Tyrrell was at Zandvoort in Holland to see the debut of the Ford-Cosworth GP engine has never been explained; but the important thing is that Ken was there. He saw Graham Hill lead some of the race in one of two factory Lotus 49s, and Jim Clark win in the other car, after Hill's retirement. This was the occasion on which Ken had his order off to Cosworth by eight o'clock the next morning, even though he couldn't see the £21,000 that was needed to pay for them. Jackie Stewart was obviously going to move away from his Formula 1 drive at BRM, and Ferrari looked like signing the Scot. Stewart thought that the Italian firm were offering a very competitive car for the coming season. Despite this, Ken approached Jackie to drive a Ford-powered Formula 1 car for him in 1968.

Jackie swiftly said: 'You can't afford me.'
Ken parried with: 'How much?'
Equally speedily JYS retorted: '£20,000.'
'It's a deal,' quoth Mr Tyrrell, still wondering where he could get the money.

Ken's persistence had proved its worth in securing Stewart, but he still needed some help to get the project off the ground. Matra had agreed to loan the necessary Formula 1 chassis (even though they were developing their own twelve-cylinder engine, which was what eventually forced the split between this successful partnership) and Bill Bailey of Dunlop courageously agreed to provide finance and racing tyres after a four-minute meeting with Ken and Jackie.

Tyrrell's straightforward approach to men at the top had paid off when the deal was so nearly jeopardized by Stewart's inclination toward Ferrari. Ken had to guarantee some substantial backing for his Matra-Stewart project, and he had seen Walter Hayes of Ford at Monza in late 1967. Typically, Hayes had agreed without hesitation to back Tyrrell through the remaining tense negotiations.

So, with finance provided, Dunlop's desire to get right to the top of the racing-tyre war, the availability of the Ford-Cosworth engine and the loan of the Matra chassis, Tyrrell was able to break into Formula 1. That first year, 1968, brought him and Jackie three outright GP wins; the second year brought the World Championship with six GP wins, the Drivers' Championship for Jackie and the Constructors Award for Matra International.

A fairy tale come true? Yes, but there were problems in preparing for 1970 which the Tyrrell team tackled in two ways. Ken found that nobody wanted to sell Jackie Stewart a chassis — who needs to get beaten by their customers, after all! March Engineering provided the temporary answer, while Tyrrell held another characteristic propositioning deal. This time the man asked if he'd like to do something for Ken was Derek Gardner, a designer who had met Tyrrell through his work during the Ferguson 4-WD's brief Formula 1 life. When Gardner agreed to design Tyrrell a car he was told, in February 1970, that it must appear at Oulton Park's Gold Cup meeting in

Jackie Stewart in the Tyrrell-Ford 005 races to victory in the 1972 Canadian Grand Prix

August 1970. This precise timing meant that Ken could go out looking for sponsorship in 1971 on the basis of his new car's performances in the North American Grand Prix events at the end of the season. In fact, the car led both Canadian and USA GPs by 30 seconds before retiring, enough to convince Goodyear and Elf of the Tyrrell's potential.

I can recall two remarkable things about the Tyrrell team in 1970. First, they were the only team ever to score a Grand Prix win with the March (it still hasn't won again, and Ken keeps threatening Moseley of March that he will eventually sell his GP-winning car back to the factory at great profit). The other thing was how well the team settled into working with François Cevert, following Johnny Servoz-Gavin's instant retirement after failing to qualify at Monaco. Incidentally, there was talk of calling that first Tyrrell-Ford a straightforward Ford in thanks for that company's assistance, but both Walter Hayes and I felt that this would be something the other teams would view with suspicion, as so many of them were also using our GP engine. We also felt that Tyrrell's name should be included as a tribute to his part in the car's construction.

Since Ken has had his own car, the team's outstanding record is well known. They have already taken two World Championships (1971 and 1973) for drivers, and one for constructors (1971), and Jackie went on to win more Grand Prix races than anyone ever before, all in a car that he'd first described as 'a heap of junk'.

Obviously, things have changed fantastically in the fourteen years since Tyrrell set up to enter and prepare those F/Junior cars. Today Elf Team Tyrrell has a permanent staff of up to 25 people, capable of producing a modern Formula 1 chassis from scratch, almost entirely on the premises. The wood-yard houses glassfibre, metal fabrication and machining facilities that enable Ken Tyrrell to operate as a remarkably self-contained unit. Tyrrell himself reckons that in 1960 those loaned cars and engines for a Formula Junior cost about £15,000 a year to run, while today the cost of building his own Formula 1 cars has boosted annual running costs to a quarter of a million pounds per annum.

Ken Tyrrell's close relationship with his drivers is just one of the secrets of his success. Top, he discusses a problem with Jackie Stewart and above, one of his many rewards: victory for his drivers at the 1973 Belgian Grand Prix

Compared with other Formula 1 teams, Tyrrell's stands out in my mind for the small number of personnel involved and the resilient team spirit that has coped with worrying brake failures and, for 1974, a completely new pair of drivers. Yet Jody Scheckter or Patrick Depailler could drive a Tyrrell to a Grand Prix win this year, and I am sure that Ken is looking to this season to set the team up for the very top again in 1975.

Sponsors play a big part in success today. Elf are particularly right for Ken, getting full benefit from the association, yet without standing in the way. Goodyear have backed Tyrrell 100 per cent since Dunlop's withdrawal at the end of 1970, and this is also a no-nonsense deal that suits Tyrrell well.

One clue to those still looking for that Tyrrell secret can be found when you look at his home life. Behind every man there is said to stand a woman, and Tyrrell has the absolute support of the gentle and relaxed Norah Tyrrell, a complete contrast to the busy Mr Tyrrell. A racing pit — the small trackside boxroom about the size of a horse's stable — is a frantic place to be in during an event and practice. The sleek single-seater cars rush in with their problems, and everyone has to shout to make themselves heard, as well as having to do their own rushing around to attend to the problems and modifications that the driver needs *now*. In this sort of atmosphere, Norah Tyrrell is the rock that overlooks it all, while waves thrash below. In fact, with both Norah Tyrrell and Helen Stewart in the same pit, everyone retains a layer of civil behaviour, even during moments of crisis. Typical of Ken and Norah's approach to team spirit is their annual mechanics and associated personnel dinner, a riotous affair at which it is a tradition that a driver appears dressed as Santa Claus. Jody Scheckter has already settled into the part after Jackie's retirement.

Another clue to Team Tyrrell's success is found simply in the way that Ken does business. One of my tasks is to mind Ford's motor sport activities in Europe, and that involves dealing with all kinds of men. In the competitive world of mechanical sport, it is hardly surprising that some of these people exhibit the desire to take all, both on and off the track.

Ken is just as hard-nosed as the next man, but he is easier to deal with, because you know that he will make an honest agreement. I think the stories I've mentioned clearly illustrate how Ken goes straight for what he wants, be it a driver, car, engine, designer or business relationship with a sponsor. While some of the top men in the sport will go for the last penny that is available today, Tyrrell will often be better off in the slightly longer term, just because he knows exactly what is wanted, and proceeds to get it with a minimum of fuss.

Finally, there's one thing I'm sure of: if I were a racing driver, I'd step confidently into a Tyrrell — race after race.

Jackie Stewart the sportsman

In whatever field Jackie Stewart competes he is bound to succeed for he is driven on by the same determination that took him to the top in his motor-racing career

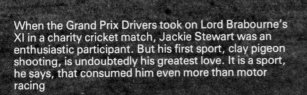

When the Grand Prix Drivers took on Lord Brabourne's XI in a charity cricket match, Jackie Stewart was an enthusiastic participant. But his first sport, clay pigeon shooting, is undoubtedly his greatest love. It is a sport, he says, that consumed him even more than motor racing

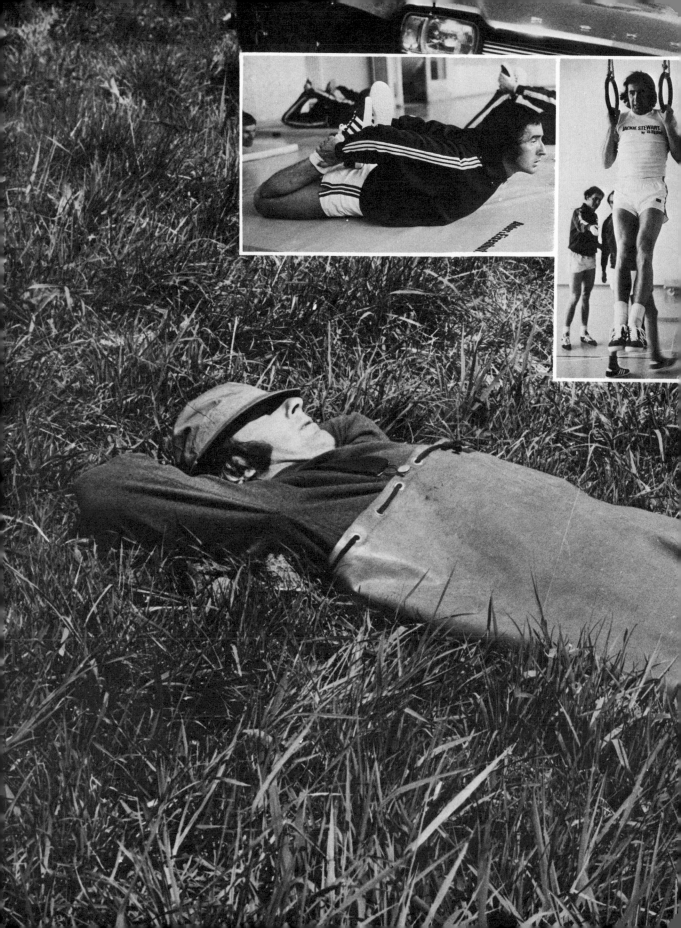

To keep himself fit, he would take part, as often as he could, in astronaut's training for Grand Prix drivers at St Moritz, opposite. But when it is time to relax, he enjoys nothing more than a day's fishing in Scotland

Why I stopped racing

by Jackie Stewart

One by one I watched close friends die on the race track, yet each time I slipped back into the cockpit, away from the harsh glare of the awkward truth. Then I saw the strain on Helen and the boys, and I made my decision

'Getting married and retiring are two of the most traumatic experiences that a man goes through in life,' says Jackie Stewart pictured below on his wedding day in 1962 and opposite with Helen and sons, Paul and Mark, on the day he announced his retirement

Getting married and retiring are two of the most traumatic experiences that a man goes through in life — that is to say if he gets the opportunity. Both require a great deal of thought and with both there is always the fear that the sacrifices made at the time will outweigh any possible benefits in the future.

I remember being driven to the church for my marriage in 1962. I turned to my best man and said: 'God, I hope I'm doing the right thing!' Even at that late hour I wasn't certain. I had only known Helen for six years. What if she changed? What if I changed? What if we wanted to get out of it? Happily, all my fears, at least at the time of writing, have proved unfounded!

My retirement was in a way equally emotional. Once again I experienced the concern of whether I was doing the right thing in the weeks leading up to 14 October 1973 when I was officially to announce my retirement as a racing driver. I had come to my decision many months before, but I suppose it was a little like a smoker who had decided to give up smoking: it's one thing to have taken the decision, quite another to bring it out in the open and announce it officially to family and friends.

Motor racing is in many ways a strange sport. For a driver it offers a unique assortment of experiences and sensations, so extreme at times that you wonder if they can all come from the same world. When the racing bug bites, it is often impossible to shake it off; it seems to infect your entire body and somehow gets into your bloodstream. It can be the world's most exhilarating sport, but it can also be the most cruel.

I cannot remember when I first thought of retiring. Whenever I was asked when and if I was going to retire, I would say that I was sure that one morning I would wake up and say to myself: 'I don't want to race again.' But in fact there was no sudden awakening, as I had hoped. The obvious first time should have been when Jim Clark died on 6 April 1968. Jimmy had been such a good and close friend, but somehow his death had been almost impossible to accept. It had been a freak accident. It didn't seem to apply to me.

What happened in the next three months should also have made me think about retiring. Almost to the same day of the month, a driver was killed in April, May, June and July, in each case, a driver whom I had known well and with whom I had raced regularly. Yet at the time, I never thought of retiring for a moment. I admit to being nervous after the second month, and I remember being aware of my poor performance in the French Grand Prix at Rouen on 7 July when Jo Schlesser so tragically lost his life. But retiring? No!

I suppose it could be said that I was still naïve and intoxicated by the candyfloss world that racing can seem to be, but I'm sure the thought never actually crossed my mind. At the end of April 1968 I broke my wrist while practising for a Formula 2 race in Madrid, and spent the rest of the season getting over that problem. I suppose I was occupying my mind as actively as possible in other ways.

The year 1969 brought me the World Championship for the first time. Since March 1964 I had driven each year for Ken Tyrrell, first in Formula 3 then in Formula 2 during 1965, 66 and 67. Ken had put together a Formula 1 team for the 1968 season. We had done well, winning three Grands Prix and narrowly missing the World Championship. But 1969 was our year — six victories in Championship races and the world title by Monza. Retirement never entered my mind.

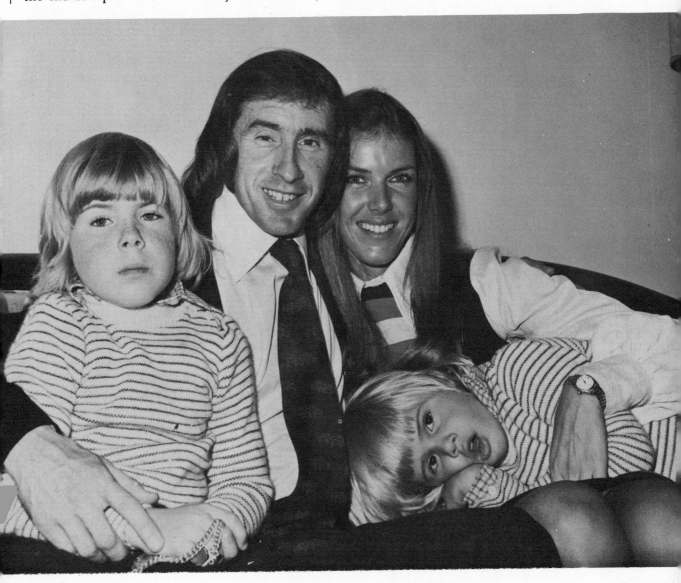

However, my first taste of real pressure came that year, not so much from the race track, as from demands on my time now that I was successful. By virtue of my being World Champion, both Helen and I were obliged to appear at lunches and dinners in almost every country in the world between the end of October and March of the following year. Perhaps that was the first time I wondered if it was all worthwhile.

The following year was a crucial one. We had designed a new car, which, though good, was not good enough. But that was the least of it. Three accidents occurred which were to affect my thinking about motor racing. All three inflicted different kinds of pain.

The first blow came when Bruce McLaren was killed while testing a car of his own conception at Goodwood on 2 June 1970. I was standing on a street corner outside a restaurant in Paris when a friend told me the news. I couldn't believe it. Bruce was one of the most conservative drivers in the business. Yet, sure enough, something mechanical had gone wrong, and Bruce's car had crashed heavily, and at high speed, on the main straight. Helen and I had known Bruce and his wife, Pat, since I had started to drive a Cooper for Ken Tyrrell in 1964. Bruce had been the number one driver for the Cooper F1 team at that time, and had given me a great deal of help when I needed it most. One of the nicest men in racing had been lost.

Two weeks later, during the Dutch Grand Prix, one of England's finest racers died in a horrendous accident at Zandvoort race track. As I drove round I could see a car on fire. Then I saw Piers Courage's helmet lying on the track, so I knew whose car it was. The P.A. system announced that the driver had escaped, and so my pit gave me a signal that Piers was OK. It was only when the race was over that I was told that Piers was dead. This was the first time that I was to see pain and suffering at close quarters.

Helen had seen the fire from her position in the pits, and her lap chart told her it was Piers who had crashed. She had immediately joined Sally, Piers's wife, and was even more directly involved than I was. She left the track with Sally, and went back to our apartment at the Bouwes Palace Hotel to get Sally away from the track and the crowds of people. She had packed Piers's and Sally's bags in their room, so that Sally could fly out to London that same night with Jochen and Nina Rindt. It was the first time I was to see Helen being brought into this side of my life.

Jochen Rindt crashed on 5 September 1970, the day before the Italian Grand Prix — the race in which he would surely have emerged as 1970 World Champion. In the weeks following Jochen's death, I was to see the effect, in my own home, on my own children, that such a tragedy could bring. Both Piers and Jochen were close friends of our children, as well as of ours. Piers stayed with us regularly, and the Rindt household was close by.

It is a strange experience continuing to do something by choice that has taken the lives of your close friends and which, in the eyes of others, is so obviously dangerous. It is difficult to explain to those you love why you want to go on doing the same thing, exposing yourself to the same dangers that have so devastatingly destroyed the homes and the families they know so well.

The easy thing to do is to avoid looking at reality, to run away from it. And the easiest way to escape is just to slip back into the cockpit of a racing car. Once in there and on the track, all the awkward questions are forgotten. You are anaesthetized: no more pain, no more conscience, no more guilt. The driver is in his own special world, concentrating on the job in hand with no time at all for outside distractions. Only occasionally does he come out of this carefree world, and then it's so very easy to reach for another escape.

My own escape was at hand; 1971 brought a busier season than ever before. I competed in the North American CanAm series of races, as well as the Grand Prix season. From June to October I was commuting once a week to North America from Europe, simply to race. I ended up with a duodenal ulcer, but I did win two CanAm races, finished third in the series and won the World Championship. With the constant time and zone changes I had become numbed, and what Helen called 'a vegetable'. The repercussions of winning the Championship did not allow me to put my feet up when

the season ended, so by the end of the year I was a very tired wee boy.

My ulcer was discovered to be bleeding which came as no surprise to some people. It meant six weeks without racing and more time than I had ever had before with Helen and my two sons. It was great. I was heavily sedated, very relaxed and enjoying what was a new experience. Then, on 11 June 1972 — my birthday — Jo Bonnier was killed at Le Mans. Once again it was a tragedy close to home. Jo had been more to do with choosing Switzerland as our home than anyone. His two sons went to school with Paul and Mark, and I took space in Jo's office complex. He was also the man who had worked harder than any other in the interest of safety in motor racing, and now he had been killed.

It was in 1970 that giving it all up first really entered my mind. Even then it was no more than a possibility. Helen had been hurt by Jochen's death but somehow, perhaps because it was near the end of the racing year, we both seemed to mend before the next season got underway. But I do remember that that was the first time I wondered if I could bring myself to retire. What would I decide to do? Perhaps I needed more courage to retire than to carry on; anyway I slipped back into the cockpit, away from the harsh glare of what had become an awkward truth.

Yet after Jo Bonnier died the pressure increased. Helen had always been wonderful. Never once did she ask me to give up, but I could now see that the strain was beginning to tell. The effect could be seen in Paul and Mark, too. They were at the same school as Jochen's daughter, Natasha, and the two Bonnier boys. Paul and Mark came home one day and asked Helen when *their* Daddy was going to be killed, because *all* racing driver daddies got killed. They were very upset because they loved me and didn't want me to go away.

I worked over the facts in my mind for some time; the most confused period for me was between February and April 1973. I thought I knew what I wanted, but I wasn't sure. Finally it all came together. I arranged a meeting with Walter Hayes and John Waddell of Ford Motor Company on 5 April. I committed

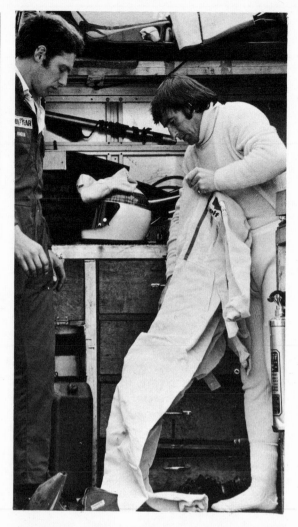

myself to retiring after the United States Grand Prix on 7 October. No one else was to know except Ken Tyrrell — least of all Helen. I did not want her to be involved in a ten-green-bottles-sitting-on-the-wall scene, waiting for the last green bottle to come down at Watkins Glen in October. The next day, 6 April, I was driven by Ken Tyrrell from London to his workshops in Surrey, and this gave me the chance to tell him of my decision. I was happy to get it off my chest.

However, about a month later I became more distressed than I ever remember being in my life. I went to the Indianapolis 500 to do the television coverage for ABC. I couldn't even recognize what my problem was. I was totally lost. I desperately needed someone to talk to, but there seemed no one I could confide in. Finally I chose to see Father Stan

Easty. Father Easty is an Anglican priest who enjoys motor racing and comes to as many races as he can. I found that he was in fact in Indy for the race. I was in luck: normally he lives hundreds of miles away in Nags Head, North Carolina.

He was with me within the hour. We sat in Room 139 at the Speedway Motel — a stone's throw from the track — and talked over my hopelessly mixed-up feelings. I had never been a religious person. I believed in God, but I would never at any time have considered myself religious. But what he finally did was to pray to God to take me and help me. Whatever happened in that room I don't know, but something came out of me, or something went in, because it was like having an unbearably heavy weight — which had been slowly dragging me down and drowning me — cut

loose. I knew that I could carry off what I most wanted to do: to finish the season and retire to be with Helen and the boys.

My motor racing has been a wonderful experience. If I had the chance to live my life again, I would not change a thing. The personal pleasure which I have been allowed to enjoy has been so intense that it has often frightened me. Motor racing has projected my life into a kaleidoscope of colour, movement and sensation, which I honestly feel has magnified my appreciation of living far beyond what would have been possible had I done almost anything else. To have lived so vibrantly and experienced so much by the age of 34 has been a great privilege. I wish for my fellow participants in the sport that they also have the capacity and the time, as I had, to appreciate the full flavour of perhaps the

world's most exciting sport.

Like most things in life, however, the finest do not come cheaply. In my thirteen seasons of racing I have lost many friends. Only nine days before I announced my retirement, for instance, François Cevert, one of my closest friends and racing companions, crashed and was killed during practice for the American Grand Prix. He was a fascinating young man with an immense capacity for living. If there were a magic wand, for me its only task would be to bring friends such as him back. That isn't possible, of course; but it is possible to remember that they were able to do the one thing which gave them more enjoyment than anything else. There are two sides to the fast-spinning coin of motor racing and I consider myself fortunate that mine came down the right way up. I am content with my decision.

Jackie Stewart shot himself to fourth place overall as
his team-mate, François Cevert, in number 6 waved him
by in the 1973 Italian Grand Prix

The greatest race

With so many victories to choose from, it would at first seem odd
that Ken Tyrrell should consider Jackie Stewart's greatest race one
in which he finished fourth

A number of Jackie Stewart's Grand Prix racing performances have been described as 'the greatest', so why should I pick a race in which he actually finished fourth, rather than one of the 25 World Championship races that he won when driving for me? Any race that includes the world's best drivers is a great race, but there are a number of reasons for picking out this performance above all the others. To put it in the most simple terms, Stewart's performance at the 1973 Monza GP in Italy was a terrific comeback drive, from nineteenth to fourth position, at a time when he had no reason to do anything more than just cruise to the finish.

Many enthusiasts would select Jackie's total domination of the foggy 1968 German GP at Nurburgring where he scored a win by the widest margin that has been seen in modern Grand Prix events, and I shall describe that event as well. But first let me show why the Monza race (which clinched Jackie's third World Championship) was such an outstanding demonstration of Jackie's unique talent.

First, we must remember that this was one of only three events left in Stewart's commitments as a driver, prior to retirement. He knew he was going to retire, and so did I. He had not told his wife, Helen, because he did not want her counting down the events until she could be sure he was away from the tension and danger of racing. Instead Jackie, or JYS (John Young Stewart) as I normally call him, had suffered the misery of counting himself down through these final events, and this had definitely affected his driving throughout the 1973 season.

JYS had not been happy with the car throughout practice sessions at Monza. It was a critical race, for it could decide who was World Champion for 1973. Some four years previously, JYS had taken his first World Championship at Monza, so the circuit had been kind to us before.

After the four practice sessions for the 1973 event, Jackie had managed the sixth fastest time, enough to put him in the third line of the starting grid. Ahead were the John Player Lotuses of Ronnie Peterson and Emerson Fittipaldi, plus the McLarens of Peter Revson (sharing the front row, with fastest man Peterson) and Denny Hulme. Fifth man was Carlos Pace in a Surtees. All six cars were powered by the Ford-Cosworth V8 engine, and Jackie seemed to have little chance of wresting the world title from the John Player Lotus driven by Peterson. Our second Tyrrell for François Cevert was eleventh fastest, instead of being up with the leaders, so Cevert was unlikely to be of much help in Jackie's pursuit of World Championship points.

Unofficial practice on the Sunday morning of the race led to an unforseen setback. On Jackie's third lap the engine went sour. This meant that we had two and a half hours before the race in which to change the engine. From my point of view this really was a shame, as, throughout the season, we had carefully preserved the engine that was now sick as the best unit we had.

Thus, JYS went into the race without the best engine that he could have had, to face up to the ultra-competitive rivalry that is a feature of today's GP racing.

The race got away with the John Player cars going straight into the lead that they were to hold throughout the race, Peterson leading Emerson Fittipaldi (which was to prove vital in deciding the Championship). JYS spent the first five laps pressurizing Denny Hulme's McLaren in a bid for third place. Then the back end of the car started to slide out of control rather more than he would have expected. On lap eight Peter Revson's McLaren passed Jackie while they were braking for the recently introduced chicanes that are intended to slow the pace at this very fast Italian track.

On lap nine JYS had to stop for a new left-hand rear tyre, as the original was too deflated for him to be able to carry on. According to my records he lost just over a minute on the leaders before he could rejoin the race.

But what a way to rejoin. In that minute Jackie seemed to have thrown off all the cares that a GP driver has to have, such as 'I must not crash and ruin my chances in the Championship,' and, in JYS's case, the thought that he had only a couple of races to do before retirement. There seemed no way in which we could finish in among the Championship points earners on this occasion — which means finishing in sixth place, or better. It was really one of those very, very rare occasions that JYS was able to say: 'The hell with it; let's go motor racing.'

On his first flying lap Jackie was a full second faster than he had been in practice — an unusual performance under modern com-

petitive conditions, when one is running with more fuel in the car and with long-distance tyres. It was the most incredible driving I had ever seen. Starting from nineteenth place he was so fantastically quick at catching the tail-enders that we decided to give him pit signals based on the gap between him and the man in sixth place.

The race itself was 55 laps of dry and sunny hard work, but by lap eighteen he was up to thirteenth place, as Clay Regazzoni's Ferrari stopped in the pits. On the next lap we measured the gap between JYS and Mike Hailwood in sixth position at 32 seconds. With 25 laps gone, JYS had his head right down and was hurling the car around in the way that already had taken him past the Shadow-Fords of Graham Hill, George Follmer and Jackie Oliver. When Jean-Pierre Beltoise stopped to have his flat tyre replaced on a BRM, Jackie was up to eighth place with more than half the race left.

So it looked as though Stewart was really trying for a place in the points as, in his efforts to close on the Ferrari of Ickx in eighth place, he had already clipped 0.2 seconds from the old lap record. By the 32nd lap our blue Tyrrell was eighth, as Jackie took Ickx going into the chicane corners.

By this stage we could measure that Jackie was gaining no less than two seconds a lap on Mike Hailwood. The former motor cycle champion was having trouble holding down

his sixth place anyway with the after-effects of a slight collision with the chicane kerbing earlier in the race. Having inherited seventh place — after the young Austrian driver Niki Lauda had a large accident in his BRM — Stewart sailed past Hailwood on lap 37 in sixth position.

Hailwood said afterwards that he had seen the speed at which Jackie was closing up. Again Stewart had chosen the chicane to overtake, but what Mike couldn't understand was where Jackie had gone after the chicane. 'Jackie disappeared so fast that I thought he'd had an accident somewhere,' he said.

Carlos Reutemann, a very fast Argentinian

In the diabolical conditions of the 1968 German Grand Prix Jackie Stewart scored a win by the widest margin that has been seen in modern Grand Prix events. Above right, he waits in the pouring rain for the second man home, Graham Hill

driver for the Brabham-Ford team, was then holding fifth place overall. JYS was having no problem in taking an average of two seconds a lap from Reutemann's advantage, but we knew that it was no easy task to get past Carlos. In fact, earlier in the year, JYS had spent many laps at the French Grand Prix trying to do just that. Nevertheless, our car closed rapidly on the Brabham, and by lap 42 Jackie was past to hold fifth place overall.

François Cevert, in our second Elf Tyrrell, was holding fourth place at this point but, by his 1973 standards, he was not having a good race . . . and he was Jackie's team-mate, so the next move looked a bit easier. In fact, it was

only seven laps after he passed Reutemann that JYS shot himself to fourth place overall as François waved him by.

Third place was taken, held by Revson's McLaren after Hulme's McLaren had bounced over the chicane kerbing after his brakes faded and he was forced to drop away from the leaders. With eight laps to go Stewart was sixteen seconds in arrears of third position, and still pressing on really well in frequent, beautifully controlled slides.

Just four laps left, and Jackie set a new record for the track at 1 minute 35.3 seconds (218.153 kph average speed), but then he'd been doing that all afternoon. The question was could he do any more? With just a lap to go, the gap was down to six seconds, but that was too much even for the sort of speed that Jackie had been showing that September afternoon. Finally he finished just four seconds behind Revson, secure in fourth place.

Yet as Stewart drove into the winners' enclosure I had an even better surprise waiting. Contrary to the expectations of many onlookers, the Lotuses had stayed in order, with Peterson ahead of Fittipaldi. If Emerson Fittipaldi was to have any chance of keeping with the Championship, he had to finish first at Monza and at the two subsequent North American events. Perhaps because Lotus Team Manager Peter Warr knew that Fittipaldi had very little chance of winning the series and because they thought Fittipaldi would leave at the end of the season, Warr gave Peterson no instruction to let Fittipaldi

by. In the previous qualifying round (the Austrian GP) Peterson had waved Fittipaldi ahead, but the Brazilian failed to finish, so it had made no difference to the final points score.

So I was able to tell Jackie that he had won his third World Championship. At first he thought I was kidding him. When he was convinced that he really had won the title, I asked him: 'Why all the aggravation in practice?' 'I just don't know, Ken,' he replied. 'The car was pretty well unchanged. It was just everything seemed right to do my best after that pit stop.'

Some time later I was talking over the race with Emerson Fittipaldi, and he reminded me of something that had impressed me even more about Jackie's performance that day. Emerson recalled that he had been trying as hard as he could to get past Peterson, yet still his pit signals told him that JYS was catching them both at the rate of one second a lap.

So that was the story at Monza in 1973, and a very fitting climax to Jackie's career.

In fact he did only one more Grand Prix for me, or anyone else for that matter, for François Cevert's tragic death prevented our starting the American Grand Prix — which would have been Jackie's hundredth event in World Championship racing.

For those who insist that Nurburgring in August 1968 was our finest performance, here are some of the details. It was our first year in Formula 1 racing with two Matra-Ford V8s — one for JYS, one for Johnny Servoz-Gavin. Jackie had already won the wet 1968

Zandvoort GP, and the Dunlop wet weather equipment was expected to show well as the weather turned nasty at Nurburgring. In fact, we learnt a very important lesson as a team: never start practice in changeable weather with items such as brake pads to 'bed in'.

We spent the first twenty minutes playing around on the short circuit with the car to make sure that new pads were fit for the rigours of the fourteen-mile German GP track. Those twenty minutes were the only period over the whole weekend that the track was dry! So when Jackie did get out, it was in comparatively wet conditions, and he was unable to snatch a time to place him with front runners.

In the conditions of rain caused by low cloud, Jackie was faster than anyone else, but that was not enough for the team. I realized that, during a later unofficial practice session, conditions had deteriorated to the point where water was streaming across the track, so I wanted JYS to go out and see the track conditions for himself. Jackie was having a meal in the restaurant, and he certainly didn't want to go out puddle hunting in the murk. It was the *only* time I ever had to ask Stewart to go out on a race track, and he left the pits shaking his head at the craziness of it all. Naturally, I was worried at the responsibility of sending out a driver and car in such conditions, but I felt it was better to spot the streams at his own pace in practice, rather than in the heat of the race.

In the event, Jackie took only half a lap to assert himself at the front of the race, despite his lowly starting position. Left behind in the spray kicked up by those magnificent tyres were Graham Hill, Chris Amon and Jochen Rindt. Amon and Hill, two of the best drivers in the world at that time, fought for eleven of the fourteen laps, but Hill (who eventually took second place) just couldn't keep Stewart in sight.

The conditions were diabolical, the low cloud reducing visibility and providing plenty of water for the track, but our car and driver seemed to take it all in their stride. Mind you, even this winning combination was a bit ruffled when Jackie found an ambulance out on the track, looming up through the murk and travelling at approximately 100 mph less than he was!

Despite that fright, Stewart had a margin of 4 minutes 3.2 seconds on Hill at the finish, and I think this must be the most commanding victory ever returned in GP racing since the early 60s and the departure of the front-engined cars.

I still rate Monza as the better performance. We had two distinct factors on our side at that wet German race — the tyres were the very best, and so were the car and driver that relied on them. At Monza the competition was much fiercer, much better equipped, and after a delay, much harder to overcome. Doubtless the point will be argued for years, and new 'greatest ever' performances put forward, but for me John Young Stewart's drive in the 1973 Italian Grand Prix showed that he deserves to be ranked among the all-time greats.

Track record of a champion

Jackie Stewart has scored more World Championship points than any other driver in post-war history. His score, over nine seasons of Grand Prix racing, totals 360 and reads as follows:

date	car	placing	points
1965	BRM	3rd	34
1966	BRM	7th	14
1967	BRM	9th	10
1968	Matra-Ford	2nd	36
1969	Matra-Ford	1st	63
1970	March-Ford	5th	25
1971	Tyrrell-Ford	1st	62
1972	Tyrrell-Ford	2nd	45
1973	Tyrrell-Ford	1st	71

Formula 1

Grands Prix counting to the World Championship

99 races
27 victories
11 second places
5 third places
6 fourth places
5 fifth places
3 sixth places
5 finishes below sixth place
37 retired
1 non-starter

14 fastest lap in the race
17 pole positions

In addition to the Grands Prix, Jackie had:
        21 non-championship races
        5 victories
        4 second places
        3 third places
        1 sixth place
        8 retired

Formula 2

        49 races
        12 victories
        9 second places
        1 third place
5 fourth places (in one race Stewart took over
        from Ickx)
        2 fifth places
1 sixth place (Stewart took over from Ickx)
21 retired (in two races in which he retired, he
took over from Ickx, see placings above)
        1 non-starter

Formula 3

        14 races
        11 victories
        1 second place
        1 sixth place
        1 retired
        1 non-starter

CanAm/Group 7

        15 races
        2 victories
        2 second places
        1 third place
        1 sixth place
        9 retired
        1 non-starter

Tasman Championship

16 races
6 victories
2 second places
1 fourth place
7 retired

USAC Formula

3 races
1 victory
2 retired

Touring Cars

Touring cars counting to the European
Championship
5 races
1 second place
1 fifth place
3 retired
1 non-starter

Other touring cars
9 races
3 victories
1 third place
1 fourth place
2 fifth places (in one race he was fourth in
class)
1 sixth place (fourth in class)
1 retired

Sportscars, GT cars and Prototypes

23 races
6 victories
4 second places
2 third places
1 fourth place
1 sixth place
4 finishes below sixth place
5 retired
1 non-starter